ADVANCE PRAISE FOR
REEFER SANITY

"A clear-cut argument dispelling the hazy myths about a dangerous drug that threatens all of us, especially the next generation."

—WILLIAM C. MOYERS, VICE PRESIDENT OF PUBLIC AFFAIRS
AND COMMUNITY RELATIONS, HAZELDEN

"Compassionate and knowledgeable, Kevin Sabet is the most important new voice in the American drug policy debate. Policymakers, parents, and concerned citizens should heed his meticulously factual case against marijuana legalization."

— DAVID FRUM, CONTRIBUTING EDITOR, *DAILYBEAST/NEWSWEEK*

"Kevin Sabet is a beacon in the confusing haze surrounding marijuana legalization. This book relies on science—not emotion or anecdote—to guide us through this complicated social issue."

—CHRISTOPHER KENNEDY LAWFORD, AUTHOR OF *RECOVER TO LIVE:
KICK ANY HABIT, MANAGE ANY ADDICTION*

"For backers of pot legalization, Kevin Sabet is dangerous, because he can't be easily dismissed as a reefer-madness-style propagandist. The marijuana reform community should play close attention to his arguments, and the prohibitionists, if they have any plans to reverse the tide, should do the same."

—RYAN GRIM, WASHINGTON BUREAU CHIEF, *HUFFINGTON POST*,
AND AUTHOR OF *THIS IS YOUR COUNTRY ON DRUGS*

REEFER SANITY

SEVEN GREAT MYTHS ABOUT MARIJUANA

REEFER SANITY

SEVEN GREAT MYTHS
ABOUT MARIJUANA

KEVIN A. SABET, Ph.D.

FOREWORD BY PATRICK J. KENNEDY, FORMER CONGRESSMAN

BEAUFORT
BOOKS

Library of Congress Cataloging-in-Publication Data

Sabet-Sharghi, Kevin A. (Kevin Abraham), 1979-
    Reefer sanity : seven great myths about marijuana / by Kevin A. Sabet.—1st ed.
        p. ; cm.
    ISBN 978-0-8253-0698-3 (pbk. : alk. paper)—ISBN 978-0-8253-0656-3 (e-book)
    I. Title.
    [DNLM: 1. Marijuana Smoking—legislation & jurisprudence—United States. 2.
        Cannabis±adverse effects--United States. 3. Legislation, Drug—United States.
        4. Marijuana Abuse—prevention & control—United States. HV 5822.M3]
    RM666.C266
    362.29'50973—dc23
                            2013014477

For inquiries about volume orders, please contact:

Beaufort Books
27 West 20th Street, Suite 1102
New York, NY 10011
sales@beaufortbooks.com

Published in the United States by Beaufort Books
www.beaufortbooks.com

Distributed by Midpoint Trade Books
www.midpointtrade.com

Printed in the United States of America

Cover Design by Jane Perini/Thunder Mountain Design
Interior design by Jane Perini/Thunder Mountain Design

DEDICATION

For Shahrzad

CONTENTS

ACKNOWLEDGMENTS

I am blessed to have had the assistance of many wonderfully generous, intelligent, and patient people throughout this challenging process. First and foremost, I am grateful to my wife, Shahrzad Sabet, for the central role she played in making this project possible. My thinking has benefited from her intelligence and clear thinking since literally the first day we met. Without her generous feedback and unflinching support, this book would not have been completed. For that and so much more, I thank her every day. Very special thanks go to my mother and father, Sohie and Zabih Sabet, who have always provided me with unwavering love and encouragement. My debt to them is too great to ever repay. I am profoundly grateful to my sisters and their families—Homa Sabet Tavangar and Alex Tavangar, Mina Sabet Bogan and Christopher Bogan, Layla, Anisa, Sophia, Juliet, and Max—who enrich all my endeavors with their sage advice, unconditional support, and matchless humor. Finally, I am indebted to my wife's family, the "Sabets of the North"—especially Afsaneh and Saeed Sabet, and Shayda Sabet—who continually shower me with warmth, affection and kindness. Their selfless love is a constant source of support.

In many ways, several aspects of this book have been in the works ever since I first experimented with drug policy back in middle school. The people who initiated my addiction to policy were Marilyn MacDougall and Brad Gates, who managed the countywide drug awareness newspaper, *The Quest*. My involvement with *The Quest* allowed me to travel to Washington DC, at sixteen, where I met Sue Thau and Sue Rusche, the two people you should blame if you don't like the fact that I work in this area today. I also owe thanks to Steve Alm, Michael Botticelli, Thom Browne, Fe Caces, Mike Cala, Tim Condon, Arthur Dean, Jennifer de Vallance, David Evans, Calvina Fay, Thom Feucht, West Huddleston, David Johnson, Chris Kennedy Lawford, Regina LaBelle, Melody Heaps, Pancho Kinney, Rafael Lemaitre, Tony Martinez, David Mineta, William Moyers, Jessica Nickel, Tim Quinn, John Redman, Tom Riley, Patrick Schmidt, Betty Sembler, Ken Shapiro, Jack Stein, Ben Tucker, and Terry Zobeck.

I am also indebted to several scholars much brighter than me for challenging my assumptions, sharpening my thinking in this area, and allowing me to learn from them: Bob DuPont, who has patiently taught me more about drug policy, politics, and program implementation than anyone else while simultaneously cheering me on with endless enthusiasm; Rob MacCoun, who taught the first class I took on drug policy at the University of California–Berkeley and showed me that policy analysis was more than just talking points; the late David Musto, for our discussions in his Yale office about drug policy history; George Smith and James Sandham at Ox-

ACKNOWLEDGMENTS

ford University, who carefully guided me through my PhD; the late Bruce Johnson, who was taken away from us far too soon, and secured my pre- and post-doc positions at the National Development and Research Institutes, despite the odds; Mark Kleiman, who, one summer, secured me much-coveted gubernatorial office space at the University of California–Los Angeles's policy school, edited my first contribution to a drug policy book, and tolerated my countless questions about drug control over several lunches he paid for; and many others, including Drew Pinskey, David Frum, Jon Caulkins, Rosalie Pacula, Alice Mead, Beau Kilmer, Peter Reuter, Mel Levitsky, Sue Foster, Keith Humphreys, Bill Alden, Tom McLellan, Sally Satel, Pam Rodriguez, Sharon Levy, Steve Talpins, Stu Gitlow, Alan Leshner, Gilberto Gerra, Mitch Rosenthal, Viridiana Rios, Art Dean, Neil McKeganey, John Coleman, and Bertha Madras. I am especially indebted to my colleagues at the University of Florida: Scott Teitelbaum, John Harden, Priscilla Spence, Debra Krawczykiewicz, Connie Pruitt, and especially Mark Gold, who is responsible for my appointment as Director of the Drug Policy Institute. You all make me wish that I could spend more time in Gainesville.

There is a small handful of people from whom I have acquired knowledge that no textbook or lecture could ever teach. The knowledge and experience I gained from working for the Office of National Drug Policy Directors Gil Kerlikowske, Barry McCaffrey, and John Walters are truly invaluable. I will always treasure the lessons I learned from these men.

Patrick Kennedy, with whom I am pursuing a new and exciting policy endeavor, and his wife Amy, along with (his assistant) Kara Kufka, must be thanked for their selfless dedication and endless patience. I am also indebted to Patrick for generously offering to write the foreword to this book.

Outstanding research assistance was provided by Randall Fitzgerald, Mari Cohen, Bradley Nelson, and Leba Sable. And in particular for patiently reading this manuscript, I thank David Frum, Sharon Levy, Alice Mead, John Redman, Homa Sabet Tavangar, Shayda Sabet, and Shahrzad Sabet. My agent Jack Jennings, who agreed to take this project on, and David Nelson at Beaufort and Eric Kampmann at Midpoint, who made publishing this book possible, have earned my highest appreciation for seeing this project through. Megan Trank, Cindy Peng, and the staff of Beaufort also deserve a big thank-you for their patience and determination.

Of course, any errors of fact, judgment, omission, and commission that remain in this book are solely mine.

Finally, I must warmly acknowledge the professionals who work on the front lines in this area—teachers, prevention workers, treatment personnel, doctors, law enforcement officials, and community volunteers. Often out of the spotlight, they are saving lives while the rest of us watch and comment from afar. Thank you.

BY PATRICK J. KENNEDY

I t was November 6, 2012 and President Obama, with whom I had forged a special bond after my father's passing in 2009, had just won a resounding reelection victory. Social issues had also been up for a vote at the polls that day. In Maine, Maryland, and Washington, gay marriage ballot measures cruised to victory. And, in two of three states where it was on the ballot, marijuana legalization was passed by popular vote. This was all happening just as I was beginning my odyssey as a private citizen to advocate for the implementation of the Mental Health Parity and Addiction Equity Act (MHPAEA) which had been the hallmark of my time in Congress.

Like most Americans, I was sympathetic with those who argued we shouldn't allow our criminal justice system to be a substitute for a public health approach to addressing the disease of addiction. I was a champion of both drug courts and mental health courts for this same reason.

I was also sympathetic to the notion of medical marijuana being available to treat people with diseases like cancer, as I had seen firsthand, in my family, the effects of chemotherapy.

The evolution in my thinking about the medicalization and decriminalization issues surrounding marijuana has taken me a long way from my early support for them in Congress.

When I had time to evaluate the movement for legalization of marijuana I realized my initial thoughts were misguided and naive. Here are the facts that speak for themselves—learned from experts who educated me on the real story of the legalization movement:

- Less than 5 percent of people in medical marijuana programs around the country have cancer, HIV, or glaucoma.
- The American Medical Association does not support smoked marijuana as medicine. Research into non-smoked components and extracts shows promise.
- Big Tobacco has been eyeing marijuana for some time now.
- While 52 percent of Americans regularly drink and 27 percent smoke, only 7 percent use marijuana. Illegality keeps prices high and use relatively low.
- Today's cannabis is five to six times stronger than in the 1960s and '70s. This increase in potency has resulted in worse health and addiction outcomes.
- One in six children who use marijuana will become addicted, and with regular use, may suffer the loss of six to eight IQ points.

My desire to incorporate this new understanding with my ongoing efforts to promote implementation of the Mental Health Parity

FOREWORD

and Addiction Equity Act has led me to reconnect with Kevin Sabet, a former White House advisor.

In this book, *Reefer Sanity*, Kevin has mastered the science on marijuana and translated it into language that politicians and the public can understand. He has successfully challenged some of my early misconceptions about this drug. The argument is fair and clear: Marijuana, though not as harmful as cocaine or heroin, is subject to many unhelpful myths perpetuated by rhetoric and conjecture. It's a drug that causes damage to an appreciable number of people who use it, and its increased potency is contributing to climbing addiction rates, especially among children.

Marshalling scientific evidence and common sense, Kevin has written the most comprehensive book on marijuana policy today. The book describes complex issues in ways all of us can understand. By debunking prevalent myths about marijuana, this book will force people to challenge their own assumptions about marijuana and consider the future of marijuana policy. We are not destined to choose between two extremes. Good policy is not about the false choice of "legalization versus incarceration."

PATRICK J. KENNEDY
Former Congressman D-RI
Cofounder, One Mind for Research
Founder, Kennedy Forum for Mental Health
Cofounder, Project SAM (Smart Approaches to Marijuana)

TIME FOR SANITY ABOUT "REEFER MADNESS"

Marijuana. Cannabis. Reefer. Pot. Whatever you call it, this is a plant with which the world has had a deep relationship for thousands of years. Marijuana has been used by more than one in three Americans living today. Most have neither crashed a car nor dropped out of school after smoking the drug. Many have found that smoking a joint is as enticing and enjoyable as casually sipping a glass of wine. And some have even attested to the plant's medical properties: the MS patient who can move her limbs more freely, or the Harvard University lab scientist who found that ingredients in the plant actually stunt cancer growth.

For the majority of users, smoking marijuana is enjoyed in the mellow company of friends without causing any major problems. And one thing is for sure: most users have never suffered the dreaded "reefer madness" that was predicted by church films of the past. All of this is undeniably true.

At a party I attended for political appointees of the Obama administration a few months after the 2008 election, I was on a guest list that included some of the smartest, most high-minded, and well-meaning people I've ever met. These people had adorned blogs and newspapers as the next "great American leaders," the wunderkinds of our day. Not all were young up-and-comers. Some were well-established professionals turned into earnest Obama campaign workers, taking leaves of absence from teaching at top universities or quitting high-powered law firms, toiling for next to nothing to help deliver the hope and change that a hitherto relatively unknown senator from Illinois was promising.

I didn't fall into either category of politicals, as we appointees were called. In fact, you might say that I earned my invitation to that party the easy way. Unlike my fellow political appointees, I was fortunate to have skipped the grueling political campaign (I've never worked for a political candidate and remain nonpartisan). Having earned a PhD in social policy from Oxford University and having worked in the field of substance abuse since 1993, one day I got a call from the nascent administration to come onboard and help craft the president's drug policy. It was an offer I couldn't refuse.

As I spoke to several of the other Obama appointees at that party—people working on the president's new healthcare plan, civil rights, and education issues—I described the work I hoped to do in the drug czar's office, but quickly drew some puzzled looks. People had heard of this office in the White House, officially titled the Office of National Drug Control Policy (ONDCP), but they didn't really

INTRODUCTION

understand what it was all about. I'm a drug policy wonk who can rattle off some pretty obscure facts about the office that Joe Biden led Congress to create in 1988. But most of these folks knew nothing about drug policy outside of maybe participating in the Drug Abuse Resistance Education (DARE) program when they were nine or ten. Interestingly, they seemed to assume that my appointment was part of an effort to pursue some form of marijuana legalization.

"Legalization is the only rational thing to do," a more self-assured appointee at the party commented. "Pot is no worse than beer. And besides, people shouldn't go to jail for it." Others chimed in, "We've waged this war on drugs for forty years with nothing to show for it. Marijuana is everywhere. And it even makes you a better driver."

Others were suspicious of me because I had served in a more junior policy capacity with the "other side"—the Bush administration (as well as a few months with the Clinton administration). To the Obama appointees I spoke with, to be against drug use was to hold a *conservative's* position, an old person's position, and—God forbid—to be a cheerleader for that lady, "What was her name? Ah yes, Nancy Reagan! She loved that 'reefer madness' baloney."

Like many Americans, however, their conceptions about the science of today's marijuana, and the wisdom of legalization, *were all wrong*. Indeed, the facts about marijuana listed in the beginning of this introduction—the history of the drug, its medical potential, and the probability of harm resulting from its use—are all true. But, when weighed against the evidence, they are not compelling reasons to legalize marijuana. Indeed, research reveals that legalizing today's more potent marijuana would significantly increase health and safety costs in society. These costs are real—but severely underappreciated—perhaps because people have a tendency to generalize their own experiences to the larger population. It turns out that legalizing marijuana is, on balance, the wrong way to go if we care about public health, public safety, and, indeed, the public good.

At that party—confronted head-on with some of today's misconceptions about marijuana—the idea for this book really began to take shape. It became clear to me that someone needed to shed light on the latest scientific findings about this drug and to sort through all of the confusion, politics, and shouted rhetoric that makes it exceedingly difficult for anyone to reasonably weigh the facts on this issue. Myths about marijuana abound.

The creation of these myths spans the ideological spectrum. During most of the twentieth century, much of the mythmaking involved hysterical attempts to demonize marijuana and its users. The notorious 1936 movie *Reefer Madness*, which was a private, semi-amateur production, not a government propaganda film, showed people going instantly insane the first time they tried the drug, killing their neighbors and having wild, uncontrollable sex. When marijuana became a staple of the 1960s counterculture, mainstream conservative elements of society reacted to use of the "devil weed" with an attitude of "lock up all the users and throw away the key." There is also no doubt that some of our nation's first anti-drug laws were motivated by the fear of Mexican immigration and of the black jazz movement (David Musto's book, *The American Disease*[1], offers an accurate account of the origin of US drug laws).

When I first met my wife, a Canadian, one of her only experiences with the American drug policy debate was having heard an American official say in a radio interview that her country's unwillingness to be "tough on drugs" was tantamount to state-sponsored murder. Understandably, she was instantly turned off by that extreme rhetoric and began doubting everything that American government agencies and officials claimed about drugs and drug policy. And from speaking to many of my contemporaries—whether American or not—I've realized that my wife's experience was typical, not exceptional.

This history of fear mongering has resulted in a lot of baggage about marijuana in our country. The imagery that comes with it—revolt, protest, anti-Vietnam War, Woodstock, and Nixon—has contributed to the reality that marijuana remains the most misunderstood of all drugs. Talk to some pro-marijuana advocates and bloggers and it quickly becomes apparent that marijuana has taken on something of a religious status among them. On the other side, hawks project in the harshest possible words their disgust for marijuana and its users. But, by and large, the legends and misconceptions about marijuana that dominate mainstream thinking today rest on the idea that marijuana is a harmless medicine, and that taxing it is the solution to both government budget woes and underground market violence. People wonder, "What is the big deal?" and "Why does the government care to keep it illegal?"

IS TODAY'S MARIJUANA A BIG DEAL, AND SHOULD WE CARE ABOUT IT?

As we were crafting President Obama's first drug policy strategy, he asked us to focus on the science and put rhetoric aside. The first thing my boss, ONDCP director Gil Kerlikowske, did in an interview with the

Wall Street Journal, was to proclaim that the "drug war is over" and that we would be reorienting drug policy toward a more balanced, health-oriented approach. Some took that as code for marijuana legalization. But it actually meant that we would use the best evidence available to address the many, complex aspects of drug policymaking. And that evidence pointed away from, not toward, legalization.

Because I served both Republican and Democratic presidents, I had a unique vantage point from which to view the development of federal policy toward marijuana. There were differences between administrations in both style and substance. In terms of our approach to marijuana policy in the Obama administration, we didn't want to repeat the harsh rhetoric of past eras. We tried to keep our focus on the actual consequences of drug use, especially the personal health and healthcare costs and consequences. Frankly, we struggled to connect with certain congressional Democrats to persuade them that this was an issue they should care about. It was a struggle because drug policy is too often characterized as a moral, or conservative, issue. Self-identified liberals do not want to be seen legislating morality. It is ironic, then, that most of our anti-drug laws have their origins in legislation pushed by Wilson and FDR progressives, and, later, by leaders like Bill Clinton and Joe Biden.

One of the first tasks we undertook in the Obama administration was to review the vast literature on marijuana that has emerged in the past thirty years. We quickly found that science has revealed more about this drug in the past few decades than it had in the preceding six thousand years. Some of the evidence is still mixed (e.g., we still don't know definitively whether marijuana, like tobacco, causes lung cancer). But one clear finding is that the drug is much more potent today than it was just two decades ago. Checking and rechecking our sources, speaking with scientists and researchers, we quickly realized that today's marijuana is a totally different drug from the "Woodstock weed" that baby boomers experienced during the 1960s and 1970s. The level of its psychoactive substance, Tetrahydrocannabinol (THC), has been manipulated by growers to intensify the "high" (talk about GMO). To make matters worse, components in marijuana (e.g., cannabidiol [CBD]) that reduce the high—and thereby reduce the risk of marijuana's health and safety concerns—have been almost completely bred out of today's street-level marijuana. With profit maximization their goal, it is unsurprising that growers have made their product as strong as possible. A policy question follows directly from this: *"What policy helps keep today's high-potency marijuana use, and its consequences, lower: some form of legalization or some form of prohibition?"* This is the question we considered.

TRANSLATING THE SCIENCE

A prevailing view is that the government cares about keeping marijuana illegal for ideological, even self-serving reasons. With marijuana illegal, the logic goes, police keep their jobs, political donors to the prison-industrial complex are rewarded, prison unions stay happy, and the liquor and pharmaceutical industries have less competition on the open market. Furthermore, it's often said that marijuana prohibition is a direct result of our Puritan heritage and the morality police. These statements have intrinsic appeal, and may even contain a kernel of truth.

It became apparent when we spoke to Americans across the country about marijuana, that parents and grandparents familiar with the less potent variety of marijuana now faced a conundrum: "I used pot and I came out okay, but does that mean I should look the other way when my children and grandchildren use it?" Many still thought of using marijuana as a harmless, essential rite of passage. After looking hard at the facts, however, there was no question: today's realities about marijuana should change everything that people think they know about the drug.

It is true that most people who will one day smoke a joint will not become addicted or have major problems with marijuana—indeed many stop after using it once or twice. But the fact that a minority of users will experience significant negative health ramifications, including a significant loss in IQ and poor learning outcomes, lung damage, mental illness, motor skills impairment, and even addiction, offers plenty to worry about. Treatment providers are already reporting that although use levels are similar to what they were fifteen years ago, more kids are showing up at their doors. In fact, marijuana is now the number one reason why kids enter treatment—more than alcohol, cocaine, heroin, meth, ecstasy, and other drugs combined. That wasn't the case just a few decades ago. This increase in youth treatment admissions is most likely attributable to the increased potency of marijuana.

Ironically, even as medical science has revealed the health harms of marijuana use, over the same period, greater tolerance of marijuana use and the idea of legalization have emerged among state officials and the general public. Why has that happened?

The vast volume of scientific evidence has not been effectively translated into information that the media and ordinary people can digest and understand. Add to this the skepticism provoked by the extreme fear mongering of the past and the pro-legalization crowd's steady drumbeat of "pot is safer than alcohol," and the result is that parents and lawmakers are confused and conflicted. There is virtually nothing out there to counter this mythmaking except the federal government, an institution of which people are increasingly suspicious, regardless of the political party in office.

Marijuana use has the potential for numerous negative outcomes, yet, as a society, we have almost become immune to any consideration of long-term risks or to have an honest discussion of the costs and benefits of any change in policy. That's one of the key messages of this book and another reason why I was prompted to write it.

DEBUNKING THE MYTHS

Myths about marijuana are not confined to the health consequences of the drug. This book confronts other difficult questions about marijuana, including: Is marijuana medicine? Are people filling our jails and prisons for smoking marijuana? Why does marijuana remain illegal when alcohol and tobacco are not? Can legalization take the profit out of violent drug cartels? Can the government benefit financially from taxing marijuana? Does Europe provide a good model for legalization? Are efforts to prevent marijuana use and treat addiction futile?

The answers to these questions are not straightforward. For some, marijuana use represents a net benefit. They enjoy a joint once in a while and do not experience any major difficulties. For others, marijuana use is a serious problem. For society as a whole, its use is a large and growing public health issue with significant costs. Any public policy has costs and benefits. But neither legalization nor a policy of throwing users in jail serves the nation's best interests. There exists another way that eschews both legalization and incarceration.

In 2012, voters in Colorado and Washington were persuaded otherwise. Several million dollars worth of ads and campaigning helped marijuana legalization initiatives there pass with 55 percent of the vote on election night. (It is worth mentioning that a similar, poorly worded legalization measure failed in Oregon, where proponents spent no money.) What will result remains to be seen, especially because marijuana is still illegal under the federal Controlled Substances Act (CSA). As of this writing, one thing has become very clear: the new Pot Entrepreneurs have arrived. In Colorado, a new marijuana tourism company emerged—My 420 Tours (referring to the numerical reference for marijuana that started in 1971, when high school students would gather to smoke at 4:20 in the afternoon)—promising to "pick visitors up at the airport, connect them to a pot-friendly hotel, set up hash-making demonstrations and dispensary-grow tours, and provide them with tickets to cannabis-themed events and concerts."[2] A *Forbes* magazine March headline read "Meet the Yale MBAs Trying to Tame the Marijuana Industry." The story detailed how a private holding company had raised $5 million in one year in order to try and "create a mainstream brand around cannabis."[3] Bars, cafés, and private clubs have already emerged to facilitate the use of marijuana.

INTRODUCTION

Voters in those states were sold a false dichotomy of legalization versus incarceration. In this book, I argue that we should not legalize marijuana with all of its attendant social costs, nor should we damage the future prospects of marijuana smokers by prosecuting and jailing them. Rather, I contend that we should shift our emphasis to education about the newly revealed health dangers of marijuana use. We should also invest seriously in interventions and treatments targeted to those users who find they are unable to quit on their own. We do not need to penalize people for smoking small amounts of marijuana, saddling them, for example, with criminal records that hinder employment or access to public benefits. And for the truly sick who do not respond to traditional medications, the beneficial components of marijuana should be made safely available through doctors and pharmacies. Before we go ahead and legalize marijuana, we ought to try these kinds of evidence-based reforms first.

In the Obama administration, we determined that a policy of marijuana legalization would pose too many risks to public health and public safety. We asked ourselves, *"Do the benefits of legalization outweigh the potential risks?"* This book contains the information we used to get our answer.

MARIJUANA IS HARMLESS AND NONADDICTIVE

"Cannabis is one of the safest drugs ever in pharmacopeia. Period." —*Allen St. Pierre, Director of the National Organization For The Reform of Marijuana Laws (NORML)[1]*

"Here [with respect to marijuana] we have a drug that is not like opium. Opium has all of the good of Dr. Jekyll and all the evil of Mr. Hyde. This drug is entirely the monster Hyde, the harmful effect of which cannot be measured." —*Harry J. Anslinger, First Commissioner of the US Treasury Department's Federal Bureau of Narcotics, 1930–62.[2]*

A s dramatic turnarounds in public policy go, "Cannabis: An Apology," a headline from 2007, provides a sort of milestone in the international debate over marijuana safety and making marijuana legal. *The Independent*, a major London newspaper, had campaigned for a decade on its editorial pages to legalize marijuana use in Britain on the grounds that it was a relatively harmless substance.

In response to the newspaper's pre-2007 campaign to rally public opinion in favor of legalization, about sixteen thousand people marched to London's Hyde Park to demand legal access to marijuana. The British government reacted by downgrading its legal status to "Class C," a category of drugs whose users receive fewer penalties than "Class A" or "Class B." All of the public policy momentum seemed to have swung behind the pro-marijuana bandwagon.

Then something happened on the way to the coronation ceremony for marijuana as a completely legal substance in Britain. Editors at *The Independent* began reading the accumulating medical science evidence about the drug, while taking note of government health service statistics, which showed that the number of young people in Britain needing treatment for marijuana addiction had doubled in just one year, from 2005 to 2006. These revelations shook up some previously rigid assertions.

"In 1997, this newspaper launched a campaign to decriminalize the drug. If only we had known then what we can reveal today," began the paper's March 18, 2007 apology to its readers. "There is growing proof that skunk [English slang for today's high-potency marijuana] causes mental illness and psychosis."

Citing research showing that the amount of THC, the main

psychoactive ingredient in marijuana, had increased twenty-five-fold since the early 1990s, the newspaper noted how this tremendous change in potency had undermined all previous assumptions about how potentially harmful to our health it is. The paper identified and quoted medical specialists who had once backed relaxing marijuana laws but who now had also changed course. For one, Professor Colin Blakemore, chief of Britain's Medical Research Council, had changed his mind because "the link between cannabis and psychosis is quite clear now; it wasn't 10 years ago." I had debated Professor Blakemore at Oxford University's Union a few years before—you can imagine how shocked I was to read his retraction.

A second specialist quoted by the newspaper, Professor of Psychiatry Robin Murray of London's Institute of Psychiatry, estimated that "at least 25,000 schizophrenics in the UK could have avoided the illness if they had not used cannabis."[3]

In the United States, similar changes of mind had been unfolding among many medical authorities concerning the safety of marijuana. To cite just one example, Dr. David E. Smith, founder of the Haight Ashbury Free Medical Clinic in San Francisco, had been a regular marijuana smoker from the 1960s until 1988, when "I smoked my last joint and fully embraced a 12-step program of recovery," as he explained in a 2010 column for the CNBC website.[4]

This veteran of the drug culture saw firsthand how marijuana could produce dependence and "significant health problems" in subgroups of susceptible youths and adults. He came to the conclusion that "marijuana is a dangerous and debilitating drug. Like those of tobacco, many of its deleterious effects are long-term and long-lasting. The nature of the drug promotes a degree of denial that is both subtle and insidious. Individuals who have chronically used marijuana may be years into abstinence and recovery from their use before they become fully aware of the extent to which their lives have been damaged by that use."[5]

This reference to how the psychoactive substance in marijuana intensifies a state of denial among users, obscuring the drug's potential health harms, is a conundrum that's important to keep in mind. As you will discover in this chapter, medical studies now document how marijuana use affects the human brain—especially in kids—in ways that impair intelligence, reasoning, judgment, and clarity of thought.

THE "DUMBING DOWN" DRUG GROWS STRONGER

How marijuana became such a public health concern starts with the economic pressures felt by the drug's growers to increase the potency of marijuana in order to raise prices—and therefore profits—from its sale. By constantly experimenting with breeding practices and cultivation techniques over several decades, producers and growers steadily made progress in greatly elevating the levels of THC (the psychoactive ingredient) found in the oily resin of the marijuana plant's leaves and flowers.

At the University of Mississippi, a potency-monitoring project has been under way for the past few decades, measuring the concentration of THC in thousands of marijuana samples randomly selected from law-enforcement seizures. Since 1983, when THC concentrations averaged below 4 percent, potency has intensified until it now exceeds an average of 10 percent. Many marijuana samples are in the 10–20 percent range. Some marijuana samples show THC concentrations exceeding 30 percent.[6] If we were talking about alcohol, this increase in intoxication potential would be like going from drinking a "lite" beer a day to consuming a dozen shots of vodka.

One obvious direct result of this intensified marijuana potency has been an even greater corresponding escalation in emergency room admissions for marijuana-related reactions. The nationwide total went from an estimated 16,251 emergency room visits in the United States related to marijuana use in 1991, to exceeding

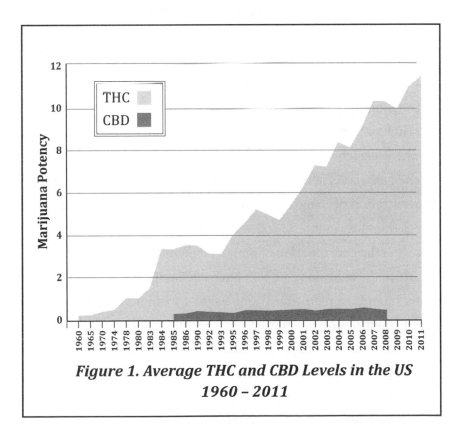

Figure 1. Average THC and CBD Levels in the US 1960 – 2011

374,000 emergency room admissions in 2008—a nearly twenty-five-fold increase in just seventeen years.[7] Interestingly, the number of users of marijuana stayed about the same during this period—suggesting that the increase in ER visits did not have to do simply with increased numbers of users. These reactions ranged from anxiety and panic attacks, paranoia, and psychotic symptoms, to respiratory and cardiovascular distress. An analysis of two large national surveys of marijuana addiction found that "more adults in the United States had a marijuana use disorder in 2001–2002 than in 1991–1992," with the highest rates among young black men and women, and young Hispanic men, even though use rates were the same for the two ranges of years studied. [8]

Today's typical marijuana sample contains up to five-hundred chemical constituents. About seventy of these chemicals are known as cannabinoids, and one of them—THC—is psychoactive. [9,10]

Human brains contain a system of cannabinoid receptors, sort of like a bleacher full of open baseball mitts available to receive pitched baseballs in the form of cannabinoid molecules. The highest concentration of these receptors is in those parts of the brain that affect thinking, memory, concentration, sensory and time perception, and the coordination of body movements. [11,12]

Once these brain receptors have been triggered by marijuana's cannabinoids, which effectively begin to mimic and then hijack some brain neurotransmitters, the resulting intoxication distorts the brain's natural chemical balance and produces distortions in thinking, problem-solving, memory, and learning, along with impaired coordination and perceptual abilities.

These adverse effects, particularly on memory and learning, can persist even after the intoxication has worn off. In other words, despite how the user might feel, he or she may continue to function below normal intellectual capacity for weeks or even months after having stopped using the drug.[13]

THE PATH TO ADDICTION

It's often said that marijuana is not addictive. The scientific evidence, however, tells a different story. Indeed, marijuana is not as addictive as drugs like tobacco or heroin, but its addiction rate of one in every eleven adults who have ever tried it—or one in six adolescents who have ever used it—should give us pause. [14]

As with alcohol abuse, many chronic marijuana users who attempt to go "cold turkey" will experience withdrawal symptoms that are classic signs of dependency. Within a day or so of initiating abstinence, the user may feel irritable, restless, anxious, or depressed; be unable to sleep; and be bothered by drug cravings. Within three days, these symptoms begin to peak, making abstinence severely challenging to maintain. [15]

Laboratory studies conducted on animals by neuroscientists clearly show how marijuana affects the reward centers of the brain in the same way that other addictive drugs do. A 2006 study in the journal *Synapse* documented how exposure to THC from marijuana produced "long-lasting changes in synaptic connections in a manner similar to other drugs of abuse." [16]

Other studies on lab animals uncovered compelling evidence that withdrawal behaviors are triggered when THC is administered twice a day for just one week, but then suddenly is withdrawn. A 2003 review in the journal *Psychopharmacology* examined numerous studies using different types of lab animals to measure the reward and dependence-producing effects of THC; it found a consistent pattern of withdrawal symptoms similar to those observed in humans. [17]

This may not sound alarming until you calculate how that figure translates into actual human lives that are harmed by marijuana. In 2010, marijuana's addiction rate meant that about 4.5 million people in the United States met the criteria for abuse and dependency, as established by the American Psychiatric Association's *Diagnostic and Statistical Manual of Mental Disorders*. According to the National Institutes of Health, there are more marijuana addicts in the United States than Americans addicted to prescription pain relievers, cocaine, tranquilizers, hallucinogens, and heroin *combined*.

Young people are particularly vulnerable to marijuana addiction, especially when they start using the drug before fourteen years of age. For this group of under-fourteen users, the risk for addiction climbs to *one in six*—almost doubling the addiction risk (of one in eleven) compared to those who start consuming marijuana later in life. [18] We can now say with authority that the earlier a person starts using marijuana, the greater his or her risk of developing dependence.[19, 20] Surveys of drug-treatment centers now find that more youths are in treatment for marijuana abuse or dependence than for the use of alcohol and all other drugs *combined*.[21]

Why does this early onset of marijuana use render a person so much more susceptible to addiction than when use begins after adolescence? It's all about brain development. Here is how the California Society of Addiction Medicine describes the risk:

"Children and adolescent brains and personalities are under

rapid development...we are certain that critical periods occur when the excessive cannabinoid stimulation produced by marijuana have significant impact on the course of brain development....As a result, they can become addicted more often and more rapidly than adults."[22]

MORE SERIOUS CONSEQUENCES FOR KIDS

As children's brain development is disrupted by chronic marijuana use, their risk for dependency accelerates. And given the ever-increasing potency, marijuana becomes an expensive public health hazard with long-lasting effects.

We can measure the impact on life development from marijuana use and its alterations of brain function in several different ways. Research shows that adolescents who smoke marijuana every weekend over a two-year period are nearly six times more likely to drop out of school than nonsmokers, more than three times less likely to enter college than nonsmokers, and more than four times less likely to earn a college degree.[23] We don't know whether marijuana *causes* adolescents to drop out of school or not, but given marijuana's effect on learning and motivation, it is safe to say that marijuana use very likely has something to do with it.

Stunted emotional development is also strongly associated with adolescent marijuana use. Females show a greater vulnerability than males to this heightened risk of anxiety attacks and depression.

A 2002 study in the *British Medical Journal,* for instance, described how researchers in Australia studied 1,601 students aged fourteen to fifteen over a seven-year period; 60 percent had used marijuana by twenty years of age. The conclusions reached by the authors should give all parents cause for concern. They wrote: "Daily use in young women was associated with an over fivefold increase in the odds of reporting a state of depression and anxiety...weekly or more frequent cannabis use in teenagers predicted an approximately twofold increase in risk for later depression and anxiety." [24]

In order to assess a young person's ability to perceive, understand, and manage their emotions while under the influence of marijuana, a team of researchers in 2006 used a sophisticated mood-testing scale to measure emotional responses in 133 college students (114 women and 19 men) with an average age of twenty-one years. Those who had started consuming marijuana at earlier ages were found to have an impaired ability to experience normal emotional responses. [25]

Both subtle and acute changes in emotional and intellectual development occur in young marijuana users because the arc of their brain's structural development becomes recalibrated by marijuana use. Brain researchers documented in 2008 how chronic marijuana use starting in adolescence significantly decreases the size of two brain areas thick in cannabinoid receptors—the amygdala by 7 percent and the hippocampus by 12 percent. One result was that young chronic marijuana users performed much worse than nonusers on verbal learning tests. Heavy marijuana use "exerts harmful effects on brain tissue and mental health," the authors concluded in the *Archives of General Psychiatry* in 2008. [26]

Memory impairment poses a serious consequence of chronic or long-term use of marijuana, and these effects can be experienced long after marijuana use is suspended. Three studies in particular make a compelling case that the "dumbing down" effect of marijuana use extends to memory skills.

Difficulties in verbal story memory, along with impairments in learning and working memory for up to six weeks after cessation of marijuana use, were found in a review of studies published in *Current Drug Abuse Reviews* in 2008. These studies were of both adolescent humans and animals. Though adolescents were more adversely affected by heavy use than adults, adults who began using marijuana in adolescence "showed greater [memory] dysfunction than those who began use later."[27]

Another 2008 review of the medical literature determined that the evidence points overwhelmingly to "impaired encoding, storage, manipulation, and retrieval mechanisms [in the brains] of long-term or heavy cannabis users."[28]

One of the pioneering studies on marijuana use and memory appeared in a 2002 issue of *The Journal of the American Medical Association* and helped to set in motion a series of subsequent studies. Nine Australian researchers compared the attention, memory, problem-solving, and verbal-reasoning skills among four groups of individuals: 102 near-daily marijuana users, 51 long-term marijuana users, 51 short-term users, and 33 nonusers who made up the control group. The conclusion: "Long-term heavy cannabis users show impairments in memory and attention that endure beyond the period of intoxication and worsen with increasing years of regular cannabis use."[29]

But the granddaddy of marijuana and learning studies came out in 2012, and astounded even the most cautious researchers. Scientists, controlling for factors like years of education, schizophrenia, and the use of alcohol or other drugs, followed a cohort of over one thousand people for more than twenty-five years to investigate the effect of cannabis use on IQ. The study found that using marijuana regularly before age eighteen resulted in an average IQ of six to eight fewer points at age thirty-eight relative to those who did not use marijuana before age eighteen. This astounding finding was still true for those teens who used marijuana regularly but stopped using the drug after the age of eighteen. "Our hypothesis is that we see this IQ decline in adolescence because the adolescent brain is still developing, and if you introduce cannabis, it might interrupt these critical developmental processes," said lead author Madeline Meier, a postdoctoral researcher at Duke University.

"I think this is the cleanest study I've ever read" exploring the long-term effects of marijuana use, Dr. Nora Volkow, director of the National Institute on Drug Abuse (NIDA), an arm of the National Institutes of Health, told the Associated Press.

The study was criticized in a paper by economist Dr. Ole Rogeberg of the Ragnar Frisch Centre for Economic Research. Dr. Rogeberg criticized Meier and her team for failing to control for socio-economic status (SES). The paper received wide media coverage. Policy analyst Wayne Hall said that the "Rogeberg study has been presented as though it was a fairly definitive refutation of the Dunedin study [but] his hypothesis has not been confirmed and that's been lost in the media coverage."[30]

When Meier and her colleagues had a chance to reexamine their results, their original conclusion was unchanged. They noted that:

"Dr. Rogeberg's ideas are interesting, but his challenge is based on simulations. We used actual data on 1,037 people to carry out the analyses he suggested. His ideas are not supported by our data....By restricting our analysis to only include children from middle-class homes, our findings of IQ decline in adolescent-onset cannabis users remain unaltered, thereby suggesting that the decline in IQ cannot be attributed to socioeconomic factors alone....Moreover, we note that our results suggesting that adolescent-onset but not adult-onset cannabis users showing IQ decline is consistent with findings in rats, and rats have no schooling or SES."[31]

A MENTAL ILLNESS LINK

About fifteen years ago, the floodgates started to open on medical research establishing a connection between marijuana use and mental illness. A lot of this research comes from countries outside the United States, such as Sweden, Britain, and New Zealand.

The first strong suggestion that marijuana use can trigger mental problems came in a 1987 study from Sweden published in the British medical journal *Lancet*. Researchers did a fifteen-year examination of 45,570 military conscripts and found that those who had used marijuana on more than fifty occasions had a much higher risk—six times higher—of developing schizophrenia relative to nonusers. "Persistence of the association after allowance for other psychiatric illness and social background indicated that cannabis is an independent risk factor for schizophrenia," concluded the four medical researchers. [32]

Subsequently, evidence from a wide array of studies began to pile up, showing that the more chronic the marijuana use and the earlier in life that marijuana use begins, the greater one's chances are of developing psychosis typified by delusional thinking and of experiencing the onset of schizophrenia, characterized by a breakdown in thought processes.

To assess the overall findings of these mental health studies from around the world, several systematic reviews of this literature have been performed to weigh the sum total of evidence. For example, a 2007 review in *Lancet* compared results from thirty-five studies evaluating the impact of marijuana use on the later development of psychosis, which was defined as delusions, hallucinations, or thought disorders. They concluded that marijuana use significantly increased the likelihood of developing psychotic symptoms. There was also a dose-response effect, meaning that the more frequently marijuana was consumed, the more dramatically the risk of developing psychotic symptoms escalated (up to 200 percent for the most frequent users relative to nonusers).[33] The survey authors concluded: "The evidence is consistent with the view that cannabis increases [the] risk of psychotic outcomes."

An even larger systematic review of studies—called a meta-analysis—was conducted by Australian researchers in 2011, for the *Archives of General Psychiatry*, using eighty-three studies to assess the impact of marijuana use on the early onset of psychotic illness. The findings were clear and consistent: "The results of meta-analysis provide evidence for a relationship between cannabis use and earlier onset of psychotic illness....[The] results suggest the need for renewed warnings about the potentially harmful effects of cannabis."[34]

Another link between marijuana and psychotic symptoms surfaced in research published by a team of eight psychiatrists and researchers in *Psychological Medicine* in 2010. They discovered that "childhood trauma is associated with both substance [cannabis] misuse and risk for psychosis." These early childhood traumatizing events can range from physical abuse and sexual molestation, to neglect and abandonment. Psychiatric interviews were initiated with 211 adolescents between the ages of twelve and fifteen to identify both their levels of pot use and any early traumatic events in their lives. The researchers concluded that "the presence of both childhood trauma and early cannabis use significantly increased the risk for psychotic symptoms beyond the risk posed by either risk factor alone, indicating that there was a greater than additive interaction between childhood trauma and cannabis use."[35]

Still another factor potentially impacting the marijuana and psychosis link is genetic. Several Canadian physicians writing in a 2012 article for *Psychiatric Times* analyzed the role of certain genes, such as the COMT (Catechol-O-methyltransferase) gene, which have been the subject of numerous studies of psychosis. This particular gene is involved with the metabolism of dopamine in the brain. A variant of this gene slows the breakdown of dopamine which may increase the risk of developing psychosis. Add to this gene variant the use of marijuana, and an even greater risk of psychotic symptoms is observed. [36]

Even if adolescents or teenagers using marijuana don't become dependent—and the majority don't—their brains are still modified by the use of marijuana. It's this modification of brain structure and function that is at the root of mental health problems later in life. As the California Society of Addiction Medicine aptly puts it on their website: "The overwhelming preponderance of scientific evidence provides adequate rationale for public policies that deter, delay and detect child and adolescent marijuana use."[37]

HEALTH HARM TO THE RESPIRATORY SYSTEM

For most people, common sense would suggest that drawing smoke into the lungs isn't natural—we weren't made to have smoke curling around inside of us—and whether it's tobacco smoke or marijuana smoke, there are bound to be some health consequences from chronic smoke inhalation.

On its website the American Lung Association has this to say about the health hazards of marijuana smoke: it "contains a greater amount of carcinogens than tobacco smoke. In addition, marijuana users usually inhale more deeply and hold their breath longer than tobacco smokers do, further increasing the lungs' exposure to carcinogenic smoke....People who smoke marijuana frequently, but do not smoke tobacco, have more health problems and miss more days of work than nonsmokers. Many of these extra sick days are due to respiratory illnesses."[38]

A wealth of medical study evidence backs up these contentions. Most of this research was conducted over the past decade. Here is a sampling, compiled in chronological order.

■ Five researchers from the UCLA School of Medicine found in 2002 that the consequences of regular marijuana use include alterations in lung function resulting in airflow obstruction;

increased prevalence of acute and chronic bronchitis; airway injury; impairment of immune system and antimicrobial activity; and a potential predisposition "to the development of respiratory malignancy" as a result of the carcinogens in marijuana smoke.[39]

■ Yale University School of Medicine researchers in 2005, reported on a survey of 6,728 adults who used marijuana and discovered a range of respiratory symptoms, including shortness of breath, frequent wheezing, frequent phlegm, and chronic bronchitis. "The impact of marijuana smoking on respiratory health has some significant similarities to that of tobacco smoking," the research team concluded.[40]

■ Writing in a 2007 issue of the *Archives of Internal Medicine,* six scientists reviewed thirty-four studies on marijuana use and lung function and found overwhelming evidence of respiratory complications from marijuana use, especially long-term use. They concluded that long-term marijuana use "is associated with increased respiratory symptoms suggestive of obstructive lung disease."[41]

■ New Zealand scientists determined in 2007, after studying 339 marijuana and cigarette smokers, that smoking one joint of marijuana was comparable to the effects on airflow obstruction of between two and a half and five tobacco cigarettes. "Adverse effects [of marijuana] on lung function is of major public health significance," the study authors warned.[42]

■ Canadian pulmonary research scientists tested 878 persons aged forty years or older in 2009, for their history of tobacco and marijuana smoking. They found strong evidence that using marijuana and tobacco at the same time "synergistically in-creased the risk of respiratory symptoms and chronic obstruc-tive pulmonary disease."[43]

HEALTH HARM TO THE CARDIOVASCULAR SYSTEM

Within minutes of inhaling marijuana fumes, a person's heart rate increases and can double, blood vessels expand, and the eyes red-den. These effects can last for up to three hours, and during this period, a variety of impacts on the heart and cardiovascular system can occur.[44] There has been evidence of marijuana-related emergency room admissions tied to cardiovascular complications,[45,46,47,48,49,50,51] but these studies have been minimal and not replicated. More re-search on this connection is needed to make any further conclusions.

MARIJUANA OVERDOSES FROM DABBING?

In the early 2010s, pro-marijuana websites and journals started discussing a term called *dabbing*. Dabbing is a practice that involves inhaling the fumes of very strong concentrates of marijuana—usu-ally waxes and oils—that have been heated. There have been re-ported overdoses from passing out after dabbing. Users can inhale so much concentrated smoke at once with this method that they pass out. Even the National Organization for the Reform of Mari-juana Laws (NORML) admits, "In the past couple of years there have been repeated occasions in which 911 teams have had to be called in due to cannabis overdoses."[52]

To make these oils, butane is often used, which is highly flammable. Butane can leave toxic solvents on the marijuana oil that is being inhaled. As the *San Francisco Weekly* reported in 2013, "The effects are immediate—and they're intense. Folks who have used cannabis daily for 30 years report, 'I am high again!' Other people not so used to the magic plant usually need to sit down for a minute or two before they can talk again. In other words, 'dabbing' is a way to ingest a lot of marijuana very quickly—and a way to get really fu**ed up."[53] Interestingly, on a website called BeyondTHC.com, an article about dabbing mentioned, "some reform honchos advised us to stop publicizing the dabbing phenomenon...."[54] It remains to be seen how popular dabbing becomes and what further dangers might be uncovered.

A MIXED STORY ON MARIJUANA'S LINK TO CANCER

Whether smoking marijuana is a trigger for causing cancer, especially lung cancer, remains an open question, though the research evidence is increasingly tilting toward the conclusion that marijuana can be a risk factor.

It is well documented that marijuana smoke contains an enzyme that converts some hydrocarbons into a cancer-causing form, one that might accelerate the production of malignant cells.[55] This is particularly important information for people with preexisting immune system deficiencies—for instance, resulting from AIDS or chemotherapy—because marijuana smoking could make them more susceptible to developing cancer or a recurrence of cancer.

A 2009 study by British scientists found "convincing evidence" that marijuana smoke can damage a person's DNA to increase their risk for developing cancer. Once again, it's a substance present in marijuana smoke—in this case, a toxic chemical called acetalde-hyde—that is shown (via modified mass spectrometry tests) to initiate the cellular damage. Writing in the journal *Chemical Research in Toxicology*, the authors of this 2009 study warned: "These results provide evidence for the DNA damaging potential of cannabis smoke, implying that the consumption of cannabis cigarettes may be detrimental to human health with the possibility to initiate cancer development. The data obtained from this study suggesting the DNA damaging potential of cannabis smoke highlight the need for stringent regulation of the consumption of cannabis cigarettes, thus limiting the development of adverse health effects such as cancer." [56]

Lung cancer, as everyone knows by now, is directly linked to tobacco smoke, so it shouldn't be a surprise that marijuana smoke, containing many more chemicals than tobacco smoke, might carry some of the same risks to lung health.

In an editorial summary of studies linking lung cancer to marijuana smoke, the *European Respiratory Journal* in 2008, offered this conclusion: "Cannabis smoking increases the risk of developing a lung cancer independently of an eventual associated tobacco exposure...some components of cannabis itself or cannabis smoke are real lung carcinogens, able to induce oncogenic molecular changes in the respiratory tract. The prudence principle should be sufficient to convince everybody that lung cancer has to be added to the list of secondary effects of cannabis smoking, along with asthma and chronic obstructive pulmonary disease."[57]

Two more significant studies showing a connection between marijuana smoking and lung cancer risk, both published in 2008, came from medical researchers in France and New Zealand. In the first, a team of twelve scientists with the International Agency for Research on Cancer in Lyon, France, did a pooled analysis of three studies of marijuana smokers and concluded: "that cannabis smoking may be a risk factor for lung cancer."[58] The nine scientists from the Medical Research Institute of New Zealand examined 79 cases of lung cancer and 324 control patients to conclude: "that long-term cannabis use increases the risk of lung cancer in young adults."[59]

Some studies, however, tell a different story. A 2006 study of marijuana smokers in Los Angeles County didn't find an elevated risk for lung cancer.[60] As *Scientific American* reported, respected researcher Dr. Donald Tashkin "interviewed 611 lung cancer patients and 1,040 healthy controls as well as 601 patients with cancer in the head or neck region under the age of 60 to create the statistical analysis. They found that 80 percent of those with lung cancer and 70 percent of those with other cancers had smoked tobacco while only roughly half of both groups had smoked marijuana. The more tobacco a person smoked, the greater the risk of developing cancer, as other studies have shown."

"But after controlling for tobacco, alcohol and other drug use as well as matching patients and controls by age, gender and neighborhood, marijuana did not seem to have an effect, despite its unhealthy aspects. Marijuana is packed more loosely than tobacco, so there's less filtration through the rod of the cigarette, so more particles will be inhaled," Dr. Tashkin said. "And marijuana smokers typically smoke differently than tobacco smokers; they hold their breath about four times longer allowing more time for extra fine particles to deposit in the lungs."

A more recent study in 2012 looked at lung function and marijuana use. Researchers looked at data from a longitudinal study collecting various measurements of pulmonary function and smoking over twenty years in a group of 5,115 men and women in four US cities. They found that "Occasional and low cumulative marijuana use was not associated with adverse effects on pulmonary function."[61] Heavier use of the drug did, however, produce a decline in lung function, and the lead researcher noted that "marijuana is clearly an irritative smoke for the lungs." Indeed, the literature on this link is mixed. The precautionary principle might apply until we have clearer or more definitive evidence.

The potential cancer risk from marijuana use might not be limited to the lungs. Several studies and reviews of medical studies have suggested that, under certain conditions, marijuana can increase your risk of developing head and neck cancers. Eight researchers at the UCLA School of Public Health investigated several hundred cases of squamous cell carcinoma of the head and neck, concluding: "Our analysis indicated that marijuana use may interact with mutagen sensitivity [which is a test shown to be associated with the risk of tobacco-related cancers] and other risk factors to increase the risk of head and neck cancer."[62] Epidemiologists, writing in the *Journal of Clinical Pharmacology* in 2002, later reviewed relevant cancer studies, noting how "several case studies were suggestive of an association of marijuana smoking with head and neck cancers and oral lesions." However, another eight-year study reviewed by researchers in the *Journal of Clinical Pharmacology* in

2002 did not find such an association.[63] Indeed they concluded that "further epidemiological studies are necessary to confirm the association of marijuana smoking with head and neck cancers and to examine marijuana smoking as a risk factor for lung cancer. It will also be of interest to examine potential field cancerization of the upper aerodigestive tract by marijuana and to explore marijuana as a risk factor for oral premalignant lesions."[64]

MEDICAL BENEFIT OR MEDICAL HARM?

We saw an interesting phenomenon play out in the twentieth century with persistent naysaying from hard-core cigarette users and industry groups trying to ignore or vehemently deny the health dangers of tobacco. We're seeing the same thing being paraded about again in the twenty-first century as the zealous pro-legalization crowd chooses to dismiss findings that challenge their "pot is safe" dogma. My hope is that reasonable people will see through the legalization smoke screen once the accumulated medical evidence is widely disseminated.

MYTH 2

SMOKED OR EATEN MARIJUANA IS MEDICINE

"We will use [medical marijuana] as a red-herring to give marijuana a good name." —*Keith Stroup, head of NORMl to the* Emory Wheel, *1979*[1]

"There is little future in smoked marijuana as a medically approved medication." —*National Academy of Sciences, Institute of Medicine (IOM) Report, 1999.* Marijuana and Medicine: Assessing the Science Base, *IOM*

I s marijuana medicine? The answer is yes, no, and maybe. Scientists have long known that like many plants, marijuana has medicinal properties. But that does not imply that to derive those medical benefits, the plant should be smoked in its raw form (we don't, after all, smoke opium to get the benefits of morphine). Nor does the potential medical value of marijuana mean that, as medicine, its fate should be left to the whims of the electorate.

No one wants to see their loved ones suffer needlessly, and there is a good case to be made that federal law enforcement should focus its limited resources on major drug producers and distributors.

Unfortunately, however, the issue of medical marijuana goes beyond simple compassion. The Food and Drug Administration (FDA), not popular vote, approves tests and new medicine for public safety in the United States. So it is troubling that some states have decided to bypass that system in favor of one manipulated by political agendas. Rather than advocating better or quicker research protocols so that pharmacists can properly dispense marijuana-based medications with consistent dosing and in a safe delivery manner, many states have bypassed the approval process of modern medicine. The result has been widespread abuses.

The federal government could certainly speed up research into marijuana's components by giving incentives to scientists who study the drug and by loosening marijuana's strict research requirements. But the current situation—characterized by the mass commercialization of marijuana and the proliferation of "rent-a-doctors" who indiscriminately hand out medical recommendations for the drug—places the truly sick at risk while detracting from the potentially promising future of properly approved marijuana-based medications.

MYTH 2

Medical marijuana as it stands today, in California, Colorado, and many other states, has turned into a sad joke. A recent study found that the average "patient" was a thirty-two-year-old white male with a history of drug and alcohol abuse and no history of life-threatening disease.[2] Further studies have shown that very few of those who sought a recommendation had cancer, HIV/AIDS, glaucoma, or multiple sclerosis.[3] We are also beginning to see a link between medical marijuana and increased drug use in some states, according to a few recent studies.[4,5]

The way to have medical marijuana is to do it right: through the scientific process, which includes proper research and investigation. Medicine by the ballot box puts public health at risk by allowing these decisions to be politicized.

One component of marijuana is already medicine. Modern science has synthesized one of the marijuana plant's primary active ingredients—THC—into pill form. This pill, dronabinol (or Marinol®, its trade name), is sometimes prescribed for nausea and appetite stimulation.

When most people think of medical marijuana these days, they don't think of dronabinol. Rather, they think of the entire leafy portion of the plant—usually being smoked, sometimes inhaled through a vaporizer, and occasionally ingested in a food item. Rather than extract the active ingredients in the plant—like we do from the opium plant when we create morphine, or from willow bark to make Aspirin—many legalization proponents advocate that smoked marijuana be used as a medicine. But smoked marijuana has never been approved by any scientific body as medicine, it does not allow for proper and consistent dosing, and it comes with all the serious attendant harms of smoking any substance.

NORML founder Keith Stroup confessed to the Emory University newspaper back in 1979 that "we will use [medical marijuana] as a red-herring to give marijuana a good name."[6] Indeed, legalization proponents have been very clear that medical marijuana is the first step toward full legalization. Their strategy is nothing less than the very clever manipulation of society's compassion for desperately ill people, burdened by serious pain and health concerns.

Let's take a closer look at what's really going on within the medicinal marijuana industry. The complex consequences of medical marijuana laws in the various states became the subject of a 2010 blog column about "medicinal" marijuana products in California, which highlighted how easy it is to obtain an authorization to possess and grow marijuana, and how easy it is to have a negative reaction when using the "medically" obtained drug.

Veteran newspaper and magazine journalist Randall Fitzgerald, who had been press director of Texas NORML during 1973–74, was curious to find out how much more potent marijuana has become today compared to decades ago, when he last ingested it. A neighbor with a "recommendation" to grow marijuana offered to share one of the marijuanan-laced baked goods that he regularly sold to local medical marijuana dispensaries.

Fitzgerald picks up the story in his blog column:

John the Baker, as I will call him, lost his construction company due to the Great Recession. He and his Napa wine industry wife were also on the verge of losing their home when they hit upon the idea of obtaining a California medical marijuana license so they could grow and sell marijuana. Getting a license to grow and consume marijuana here is easy but expensive. In rural Lake County where I reside, located about 90 miles north of San Francisco, several physicians specialize in performing medical marijuana "exams" to determine eligibility. You pay about $200 for a five-minute question and answer session. People facing severe health challenges, such as cancer, can be expected to receive automatic approval. But I don't know of anyone who has been rejected even if their only complaint was a headache, or occasional insomnia, or anxiety inspired by an overdose of reality.

The licenses for medical marijuana use expire in six months, so the prescribing physicians have a financial incentive to prescribe often and widely. One doctor I know of makes up to $1,000 to $1,500 an hour writing medical marijuana approvals. License recipients in this county can grow up to twenty-five plants for their own use. Given that marijuana has been selling lately for $3,000 a pound and a typical full-grown healthy plant can yield one pound of buds, twenty-five plants can produce $75,000 a year in untaxed income for a medical marijuana license holder. I know of at least a half-dozen "unemployed" people who make a good living selling their medical marijuana while also drawing unemployment, or state welfare and federal food stamp benefits.

Compared to the marijuana harvested and consumed 35 years ago, marijuana potency today is said to be ten times stronger. Those claims made me curious and prompted me to try a THC-laced chocolate muffin. Getting high by ingesting marijuana, rather than by smoking it, is tantamount to rocket-launching yourself into inner dimensional space without an escape hatch. Once the THC is in your stomach and gastro-intestinal tract, there is no way to regulate its effects as you can do when smoking it. Within an hour of eating two muffin bites, I began to feel the buzz of an on-rushing high washing over me like a tsunami. For the next four hours of my 17-hour stoned trip, I felt like an astronaut spinning out of control in a g-force accelerator, my face contorted and body melting like plastic until it merged with the contours of my desk chair. Freaking out could have come easily because paranoia reared its ugly head to periodically screech about how my heart and brain were about to explode. Only by repeating a calming mantra of "this too shall pass" did I manage to keep enough sanity and focus to busy myself with scribbling down the gist of a torrent of feverish thoughts about the meaning of life. Once the effects wore off the next afternoon, after an incredible 17 hours, I wanted to tell John the Baker that his product needed a warning label. He casually informed me that he typically eats two muffins—not two bites—but TWO entire muffins at a time, and somehow manages to remain functional. [7]

A year after this blog column appeared, Fitzgerald learned from John the Baker that he had stopped using marijuana altogether because he was experiencing seizures, depression, sleep apnea, and other health problems, which got better over a period of months once marijuana was no longer in his system.

Issues raised by Fitzgerald's experience with medical marijuana are multifaceted. For example, there is a liability issue resulting from major accidents and health events caused by ingesting medical marijuana, which can result in psychological or physical injuries, perhaps even death, especially if the stoned person attempts to operate a motor vehicle or machinery of any sort. I will discuss that later in this chapter. Harvard University's Dr. Sharon Levy remarked to me that "'recommending' medical marijuana for someone with a marijuana addiction at least sits near the border of malpractice. We don't 'recommend' cigarettes for nicotine dependent patients nor cocaine for coke addicts."

No one wants to see their loved ones (or anyone, for that matter) suffer needlessly, but the issues surrounding medical marijuana go far beyond the exercise of simple compassion. Let's examine, one by one, the repercussions of "medical" marijuana and the state laws that allow its use.

LEGALIZATION IS BEHIND THE SMOKE SCREEN

Rather than use the rigorous scientific testing system devised by the Food and Drug Administration (FDA) to determine what is and isn't a legitimate medicine, marijuana advocates have used "medicine by popular vote" to push their agenda, in spite of the medical evidence that smoking or eating marijuana is not a safe way to relieve the symptoms of health maladies.

In 1996, California voters approved a medical marijuana law known as the Compassionate Use Act. As Allen St. Pierre, director of NORML, admitted in a television interview, the effect of that law is that "in California, marijuana has also been *de facto* legalized under the guise of medical marijuana."[8]

Alaska and Oregon followed suit with their own medical marijuana laws in 1998, and as of this writing, eighteen states and the District of Columbia authorize the use of medical marijuana for various medical conditions, though using marijuana continues to be a criminal offense under federal law.[9]

State laws regulating medical marijuana vary widely in their criteria and implementation. Some states allow users to grow their own marijuana up to a specified number of plants, while other states only allow the purchase of marijuana from dispensaries or caregivers. City and county governments also play a role in creating ordinances that restrict where dispensaries can operate or ban them altogether, as a 2013 California Supreme Court ruling decided could happen.

Many medicinal marijuana growers sell the marijuana they cultivate to either marijuana dispensaries or to people without recommendations, some of whom live in nonmedicinal-use states. In some states (e.g., Oregon) with medicinal marijuana laws, there isn't even any age limit on who can use it. You can be under eighteen years old, which makes it more legally accessible than even alcohol or tobacco.

We already see marijuana dispensaries using fun brands and marketing techniques to promote their product. Medical marijuana dispensaries have elaborate setups with dozens upon dozens of colorful brands—Super Silver Haze or the Jeremy Lin Special—to make their product more attractive to kids and adults alike.

A recent investigation by *Reader's Digest* magazine illustrated the fact that the pro-marijuana movement is extremely well funded. The article profiled three of the largest financial backers of medical marijuana ballot initiatives—billionaire financier George Soros; the CEO of one of the nation's largest auto insurers, Peter Lewis; and John Sperling, founder of the University of Phoenix, the nation's largest for-profit university. Each of these three either vocally supports the legalization of marijuana, or has donated millions of dollars to fund both medical marijuana ballot measures and research foundations devoted to advocating for full legalization.[10]

Currently, many dispensaries are mom-and-pop operations, though there are also many dispensaries that act as multimillion-dollar professional companies. A documentary on the Discovery Channel, describing the practices of Harborside Health Center in Oakland, California—which is, by its own admission, the largest marijuana dispensary "on the planet"—showed that the cannabis plant buds that are distributed directly to member-patients are merely examined visually (vs. through approved scientific means) and handled by dispensary employees without gloves or face masks. The documentary noted that some plant material is tested by a laboratory in the Bay Area.[11]

The fear that I share with many drug policy colleagues—including a few with whom I sometimes disagree—is that there will be mass commercialization of marijuana if it becomes legal, either as a medicine or outright. Indeed, imagine what might happen when Philip Morris or other tobacco companies get into the marijuana business, as they most assuredly will if widespread legalization occurs, or if medical marijuana usage spreads to most of the states. County health departments, not to mention the FDA, will have to staff up and spend already limited taxpayer resources to maintain health and safety standards. The same spiraling of costs will occur in the nation's criminal justice system, as chapter 3 will show in detail, due to the need for extensive enforcement of minimum age use laws and driving under the influence laws.

IS SMOKING OR EATING MARIJUANA REALLY MEDICINAL?

With medicinal marijuana the concept of medicine has been completely turned on its head. Now you can pay a physician (a sort of "rent-a-doc") $45 to $200 to give you a "recommendation" to get the drug at a "dispensary." On Venice Beach in California, you can even get your "recommendation" from a bikini-clad woman eagerly directing you to a place to buy marijuana wares on the boardwalk. One can get a recommendation by claiming pretty much any illness or discomfort from an array of doctors.

The medical marijuana system in this country has become a bad joke, an affront to the concept of safe and reliable medicine, defying the standards that we have come to expect from the medical establishment. In no other realm of medicine is "smoking" considered to be therapeutic. In fact, smoking any drug is a problem because there is no way to standardize a dose.[12] Other "delivery systems," for instance, edibles and beverages, have similar problems. That is why no modern medicine is smoked and the FDA has never approved smoking as a safe delivery system.

Several marijuana vending machine companies have recently emerged in the U.S., reporting millions of dollars in revenue already.

Top: Billboard advertises where to call for medical marijuana cards. Above: People in white coats let pedestrians know about services that grant medical marijuana cards.

Why do major medical organizations like the American Medical Association continue to discourage marijuana use and frown upon the various state systems of medical marijuana? A principal reason is the FDA, which has concluded that no sound scientific study evidence has been uncovered to support the use of smoked (or eaten) marijuana as a medical treatment. The agency has, however, approved the medicinal use of certain isolated components of cannabis and related synthetically produced compounds, as briefly discussed in the beginning of this chapter.

Support for the FDA's point of view comes from the IOM, the health arm of the National Academy of Sciences, which did a 288-page report on the science behind the therapeutic effects of marijuana and disputed the idea that smoking marijuana is either a safe or effective delivery system.

The IOM report concluded that scientific data indicate the potential therapeutic value of cannabinoid drugs, primarily THC, for pain relief, control of nausea and vomiting, and appetite stimulation; smoked marijuana, however, is a crude THC delivery system that also delivers harmful substances. The psychological effects of cannabinoids, such as anxiety reduction, sedation, and euphoria can influence their potential therapeutic value. Those effects are potentially undesirable for certain patients and situations, and beneficial for others. In addition, psychological effects can complicate the interpretation of other aspects of the drug's effect.[13]

The IOM also said that in lieu of a fast-acting marijuana-based preparation, allowing terminally ill patients access to marijuana as part of a hospital-based research program with tight controls to reduce their symptoms, is reasonable. This is what was meant by "compassionate use"—*not* treating individuals with headaches or "stress," which is what ultimately transpired as a result of some creative interpretation. I don't think the IOM panel would have ever predicted that their gentle turn of phrase would spawn an entire industry, with increased marijuana use and addiction.

MEDICAL MARIJUANA "EDIBLES" CREATE NEW PROBLEMS

Edible marijuana varieties sold in medical dispensaries can be found in an imaginative range of food products—brownies, carrot cake, cookies, peanut butter, granola bars, pastries, even ice cream. Many edibles, like "Ring Pots" and "Pot Tarts," are marketed with cartoon and other characters appealing to children. It's like "Joe Camel" all over again.

Here is how a "medical" brownie—called Big Sexy's Sinful Sweets Peanut Butter Confession—sold at a West Hollywood dispensary is described by a medical marijuana patient in promotional material: it "has a different consistency from a regular brownie and isn't as chocolaty or rich, but is tasty and moist."[14] Other edibles or drinkables featured at this dispensary include pecan chip cookies

Marijuana "Pot Tarts" that come in a variety of flavors and advertise 3X strength are available as "medicine".

and pomegranate green tea. Most of the baked goods are made with hash oil or cannabis-infused butter.

A 2010 article about this dispensary in the *L.A. Weekly* claimed that the Big Sexy peanut butter brownie "has just the right dosage and the correct strain of cannabis to give a patient suffering from depression an uplifting, energizing feeling. A patient looking for a muscle-relaxing edible, say, would probably want to go with the cannabis-laced ice cream instead."[15]

Notice that medical claims are being made in this article for edible products—lifting depression and relaxing muscles. This is common in the marijuana dispensary industry. Without any medical study validation whatsoever, symptom relief claims are made promiscuously by sellers based on little more than hearsay stories from marijuana users. The medical "license" being used as a cover to make these claims was provided by voters in a referendum, rather than by the scientific process.

The potency of marijuana edibles can vary, as can a person's sensitivity, and the THC can remain in a user's system for hours after it's smoked. The Patients Care Collective, a cannabis club in Berkeley, California, advises consumers in their beginner's guide: "Most people have had some sort of an experience with edibles, ranging from magical to memorably scary. For the beginner, eating your medicine instead of smoking it can be a welcome change for your lungs, but it can also produce a wider range of effects you may not be expecting or prepared to handle."[16]

"Once you have eaten too much there is not a whole lot of remedy except to drink plenty of water. Over-medication on edibles is something best never experienced, but if it does happen, remember, you are going to be fine. Cannabis is one of the safest and least toxic medicines available."[17]

Another reason why eating marijuana can produce a more powerful high than smoking it, is explained on the website maintained by Marijuana Medicine Evaluation Centers: "When you ingest cannabis, it goes into your intestines, then passes through your liver. Your liver processes THC into a by-product called 11-hydroxy-THC, which then travels to the bloodstream and then to your brain. [The by-product]11-hydroxy THC is thought to be four to five times more potent than regular THC. This is why edibles are known to be more potent when compared to inhaled cannabis."[18]

Compounding these health problems associated with edibles, few states or localities regulate any aspect of the edible medical marijuana industry to help insure sanitation standards in food preparation, much less protect quality and standardize potency. As pointed out in a 2012 article in the *SFGate* publication, "There are few state guidelines defining how marijuana edibles can be made and sold, and a flurry of local attempts to do that has done little to change the fact that the edibles industry largely regulates itself."[19]

MEDICAL MARIJUANA EXPANDS OVERALL MARIJUANA USE

To illustrate how medical marijuana laws now service a clientele that extends far beyond the seriously ill, a study of medical marijuana users already cited found the average "patient" is a thirty-two-year-old white male with a history of drug and alcohol abuse, who has no medical history of any life-threatening diseases.[20] Most had started using marijuana before nineteen years of age.

Furthermore, a 2011 study in the *Journal of Drug Policy Analysis* discovered that, after examining 1,655 medical marijuana applicants in California, few of them had a diagnosis of cancer, glaucoma, HIV/AIDS, multiple sclerosis, or any other serious illness for which marijuana might provide some relief. [21] A similar finding came from Colorado where 94 percent of those seeking medical marijuana claimed "pain" as the reason for their medical marijuana use, compared to only 2 percent with cancer, and less than 1 percent reporting HIV/AIDS as their reason.[22]

An even more in-depth examination of medical marijuana and its relationship to the explosion in use and users came in 2012 from five epidemiological researchers at Columbia University. Using results from several large national surveys, they concluded that "residents of states with medical marijuana laws had higher odds of marijuana use and marijuana abuse/dependence than residents of states without such laws."[23]

States with medical marijuana laws also show higher average marijuana use by adolescents, and lower perceptions of risk from use, than nonmedical marijuana states.[24] This would seem to indicate that increased marijuana use results from the ease of access that comes with medical marijuana laws. These laws contribute to community norms about drug use: "If pot is medicine and is sanctioned by the state, then it must be safe to use."

Using the marijuana plant for medicinal purposes should only be about bringing relief to the sick and dying, and it should be done in a responsible manner that administers defined components of the drug in a nonsmoked delivery system with an identifiable and reliable dose. In most states where voters have approved medical marijuana laws, it has primarily become a license for the state-sanctioned use of a drug by practically anyone who seeks it.

MARIJUANA INCREASES THE RISK OF MOTOR VEHICLE ACCIDENTS

With the spread of medical marijuana, the risk to public safety has expanded in severity and scope. Unlike alcohol, for which reliable biomarkers can help determine whether a person was driving while intoxicated (the famous "0.08 blood alcohol level"), marijuana levels are difficult to interpret. There is no such standard for marijuana, and so there is a strong case to be made for outlawing any detectable level of marijuana use while driving. First, unlike alcohol, any marijuana use is technically illegal. Second, also unlike alcohol, it is extremely difficult to establish a blood concentration level that correlates to impairment levels for marijuana (or any other illicit drug, for that matter). Some fear that tests that examine levels of marijuana in the system could catch someone who used marijuana days before and is not impaired at the time of the test. However, when a motorist is stopped for a driving infraction and (a) gives the officer reasonable suspicion of being impaired, (b) fails a Standard Field Sobriety Test (SFST), (c) gives the officer reasonable suspicion of drug impairment sufficient to demand body fluids for drug testing, and (d) tests positive for marijuana, it is extremely unlikely that the positive test could result from marijuana use occurring long before the police intervened.

Still, science has shown that getting high on marijuana and operating a motor vehicle isn't much different from getting drunk on alcohol and trying to drive. Marijuana impairs a driver's sense of spatial location and sense of time and speed, whereas alcohol impairs speed and reaction time.

Either way, marijuana impairment is serious enough to present a danger to the driver, others in the vehicle, and to those traveling on the same road. According to the National Highway Transportation Safety Administration (NHTSA), one in eight drivers of a nationally representative sample of nighttime drivers was found to test positive for marijuana.[25]

This is serious cause for concern since two major reviews of all the studies done on marijuana and driving concluded, in 2012, that marijuana use significantly increases the risk of a car crash.

In one, published in *Epidemiological Reviews* in 2012, six researchers from Columbia University's College of Physicians and Surgeons analyzed studies of marijuana use and driving over the past two decades and concluded that drivers under the influence of marijuana are twice as likely as other drivers to be involved in motor vehicle crashes. Furthermore, that risk increases with higher doses of marijuana and increased frequency of use.[26]

In the second review of studies done by Canadian scientists and published in the *British Medical Journal* in 2012, toxicology information from blood tests was used and compared to motor vehicle collisions. "Acute cannabis consumption is associated with an increased risk of a motor vehicle crash, especially for fatal collisions," the research team found. "Rates of driving under the influence of cannabis have also risen in recent years...cannabis is consistently one of the most frequently detected psychoactive substances (second after alcohol) and individuals who drive within two hours of using cannabis have raised rates of collision."[27]

"There clearly is a lot of misconception about the extent to which cannabis impairs performance," Professor Mark Asbridge, a coauthor of the Canadian meta-analysis study review, told *CNN Health* in 2012. "People just don't believe it. People under the influence of cannabis often deny feeling impaired in any way."[28] The most typical observable symptoms of marijuana-impaired driving, noted Professor Asbridge, is that drivers who smoked marijuana follow cars too closely (a sign of the spatial distortion) and swerve in and out of lanes of traffic.

In a study done in New Zealand by six Australian health researchers, it was found that habitual marijuana users were nearly ten times more likely to be involved in vehicle crashes than nonusers. Those users who crashed had smoked marijuana within three hours of their accidents.[29]

Some people have tried to connect medical marijuana laws with a reduction in drunk driving crashes, theorizing that when marijuana is legal as "medicine,'" people will replace their alcohol use with marijuana use. Two US economics professors, writing in a 2011 discussion paper for a German research center, the Institute for the Study of Labor, came to this conclusion about the link between traffic fatalities and medical marijuana laws. They concluded that in the medical marijuana law states they examined, a nearly 9 percent decrease in traffic fatalities occurred, apparently due to drivers substituting marijuana for their normal alcohol consumption once medical marijuana laws are in place.[30]

My reading of their analysis uncovered several flaws. Comparing state alcohol crash fatality statistics to those associated with marijuana use, the authors of this research failed to adequately take into account that the numbers of alcohol crash fatalities were already decreasing before the introduction of medical marijuana laws in any of the states they examined. This was a consequence of education campaigns and tougher laws on drunk driving.

A second and more serious flaw in their research was that the economists studied statistics in Rhode Island, Vermont, and Montana "before" (1999–2003) and "after" (2005–9) the introduction of medical marijuana laws, which doesn't fairly represent the entire spectrum of states and their medical marijuana laws. For example, in 2009, both Vermont and Rhode Island had less than three hundred members registered in their medical marijuana programs and no medical marijuana dispensaries. The third state they looked at,

Montana, had only 6,000 members when their study period ended.

Work done by Rosalie Pacula showed that medical marijuana state policies are not uniform in their effects—areas with active dispensaries have countervailing forces that might offset negative impacts of medical marijuana on recreational use of marijuana or alcohol.[31]

In fact, there is some evidence that increased medical marijuana laws are correlated with increased crashes. In Colorado in 2007, the year after the state allowed medical marijuana dispensaries, 28 percent of the drivers who tested positive for drugs had ingested marijuana. By 2010, after the number of dispensaries increased dramatically (and was accompanied by mass commercialization), that rate climbed to 58 percent. And from 2005 to 2010, there was a doubling in the number of "drug recognition experts" (these are highly trained officers who can detect drug use among drivers) whose evaluations came up with a result of marijuana as a drug involved.[32] Also in Colorado, emergency room admissions among kids rose from zero to fourteen in the two years when medical marijuana proliferated. The *Denver Post* in 2013, reported on "pioneering studies of ER charts by Colorado doctors [that]show looser pot laws leading to childhood poisonings, often from mistakenly eating tantalizing 'edibles' like gummy worms or brownies."[33]

OTHER COSTS OF MEDICINAL MARIJUANA

Readers periodically respond to my newspaper columns and blog posts with stories of their own experiences with marijuana and marijuana policies. One letter from Ed, a California resident, concerning his state's medicinal marijuana law and some of its unforeseen consequences deserves to be published verbatim. Here it is:

> I am dealing with a disaster in California. I am being forced to move from an apartment building I have lived in for over 15 years due to the fact that even behind my closed doors and closed windows, I am constantly inundated with pot smoke. This exposure has caused me some quite severe headaches. The amount of smoke within my own walls is intolerable. The property owner is not taking action against the tenant and [at] the last visit by Police, the Police told me it is not their problem. The bigger issue, there is no guarantee that I will not have to go through this whole issue again when I move to another location.

> Concerning the guilty tenant -
> - This tenant has distributed pot to other tenants, including minors.
> - Has pot parties in his apartment.
> - On record with a Veterinarian, poisoned a neighbor's pet with medical marijuana drops.
> - On police file, was using a kid on a bicycle to deliver pot to this building.
> - Any peaceful confrontation by me with this tenant has resulted in assault, non-stop threats, and even this tenant trying to force his way into my home one evening. This resulted in a call to police. Again, police took no action. They did not even take a single note.

And all in the name of medical marijuana, this person is free to do all of this. Police refuse to act, there is nothing the DEA [Drug Enforcement Administration] or FBI will do in this situation, and the owner of this property that I have paid rent to for over 15 years is of no assistance. I'm not sure how much I can blame the owner. In the past I had a letter placed on my door from a lawyer about another former tenant. The letter threatened to sue me since I was discriminating against someone with a disability because I tried to get the tenant to keep his pot smoke to himself. Not certain what that disability could have been! I suspect the owner may be dealing with similar threats at this time.

The shortsightedness of our lawmakers to allow for this free for all, and to not put any protections into the laws for non-smokers and for the protection of the homes of people, is just no longer acceptable. I've written my lawmakers, sent emails to the police trying to get their stance in writing...nothing. In the meantime, here in California I hear kids walking around bragging about how pot is legal. Not too long ago I caught a couple of kids on the patio of this apartment building smoking pot. I told them to leave or I would call the police. Their response—"Go ahead, it's legal." I didn't bother explaining to them their mistaken assumption (or the part about trespassing) since they left without incident. But, this is what medical pot has left us. So many parents that try to raise their children properly, and our own government is guilty of sabotaging that effort.

The current tenant is 100% in violation of Federal

Law and his acts as pointed out above give him no legal claim to be in possession of a California Medical Marijuana Card. Distribution, using with or in front of minors, etc. are all disqualifications for someone to be in possession of such a card, by law, in California. Yet, there is not a person to go to, to resolve this very serious issue.

As voters in California, we were all lied to as to what Medical Pot was all about. Glaucoma patients, cancer patients, etc., all paraded about before the vote. The intention of the law, unknown to most voters was, "medical" pot was going to be allowed for anyone with any "ailment," and you as a nonsmoker being affected by these "patients," will have no right to protect yourself, your family, or your home.

Another letter from Anita describes the despair of a mother fearing for her children's safety:

I was frantically searching the web for information against medical marijuana when I found you. I hope you can provide some helpful advice. I am a divorced mother of children 16 and 13. I recently found out that my ex-husband and his live-in girlfriend are both cultivating, dispensing and using this so called "medicinal marijuana." The Department of Children, Youth, and Families (DCYF) ended up getting involved after my eldest daughter informed a hospital worker of the goings-on. DCYF has stated in short that this is all legal even with 4 children in the home, one being under the age of 3. My daughters have told me horror stories, which involve cooking with the product, cutting the product, and drug deals in the front yard. I filed an emergency order in court to suspend visits, only to be denied. I don't see how it can be legal to be a gun-owning drug dealer with children. I am beside myself and unsure how to pursue this matter other than contacting every state "rep" and agency to complain.

This law must be modified before the worst happens. Next it will be Compassion Centers opening within school zones and placing advertisements on local TV. I've already found craigslist.org advertisements. I don't want my children or any other child to think smoking marijuana is okay. There are proven studies that indicate marijuana can interfere with a child's development. My ex-husband of 12 years is growing/using in a home with children between the ages of 2–16. My girl's playroom was turned into a pot farm. I'm sure this is all unclaimed income as well.

It's hard enough to tell my 16-year-old she shouldn't be smoking, her excuse is Daddy does it and, more, he is supported by RI Law. I wish I could articulate to you how serious this issue is without sounding frantic, but quite frankly, I am. Unfortunately, I've found myself entangled in a battle I didn't choose to create. I've been told by every state agency there is nothing that can be done. I'm beside myself, and find no other response but to advocate for change.

DO FEDERAL AGENCIES SUPPRESS MEDICAL MARIJUANA RESEARCH?

This is a myth I hear often when I travel across the country. The gist of the claim is this: agencies of the federal government only finance the study of marijuana's harmful effects, and the government actively seeks to suppress research showing the potential medical benefits of the drug.

From my service as a drug policy adviser to three administrations—Clinton, Bush, and Obama—I knew this wasn't true. But I investigated the question further immediately after leaving government. I found that in the period 2007–11, the National Institutes of Health provided over $14 million in funding for cannabinoid science research.

These taxpayer funds were used to investigate the potential for cannabinoids from cannabis to treat the following list of diseases and conditions: pain, cancer (lung, breast, and prostate), diabetic neuropathy, Tourette's syndrome, irritable bowel syndrome, multiple sclerosis, brain damage, depression, glaucoma, Alzheimer's disease, stroke, autoimmune hepatitis, ALS, viral infection, liver disease, cardiotoxicity, HIV/AIDS, schizophrenia, Crohn's disease, bipolar disorder, posttraumatic stress disorder, anorexia nervosa, fibromyalgia, and many others. Add to this list of government-funded research eighteen studies of marijuana and medical maladies assisted by NIDA.

From what I found, it was clear that if a proposed study of marijuana had a high-quality trial design and experienced investigators, it would likely receive approval for funding by federal agencies. Not only that, agencies such as NIDA and the DEA have cooperated with independent researchers by providing marijuana samples for testing. The Center for Medicinal Cannabis Research at the University of California-San Diego, for example, reports that fifteen of its clinical (human) studies of marijuana received samples from NIDA with DEA license approval. Interestingly, many of these studies were halted because "patients" smoking marijuana only for "medicinal" purposes couldn't be recruited for or retained in the studies.

MEDICINAL ALTERNATIVES TO SMOKING ARE EFFECTIVE

No one should need to smoke or eat marijuana in order to derive its potential therapeutic effects. As I wrote earlier, we don't smoke opium to reap the benefits of morphine, or chew willow bark to get the benefits of aspirin.

What most people considering the use of medicinal marijuana don't realize is that it's possible to extract the therapeutic components of the plant and deliver them in a safe, nonsmoked form.

There are several medications on the market today that are cannabinoid or cannabis-plant based, and another is coming through the FDA approval pipeline. Their effectiveness for treating a range of health problems—from pain and nausea to the symptoms of multiple sclerosis—has been demonstrated in clinical trial studies.

Dronabinol was the first oral cannabinoid preparation, approved by the FDA in 1985, to treat nausea and vomiting from cancer chemotherapy. Sold under the brand name of Marinol (produced by Solvay Pharmaceuticals, Belgium), it has also been used to treat weight loss in AIDS patients. Study results on effectiveness have been mixed, but mostly positive. At doses of ten, fifteen, and twenty milligrams, some studies have found it beneficial in reducing cancer pain. Clinical trials of its use with multiple sclerosis patients found little improvement in reducing spasticity, but measureable improvements in spasm, pain, and sleep quality.[34]

Nabilone (US brand name Cesamet, produced by Valeant Pharmaceuticals International) is another synthetic cannabinoid, also used to treat the nausea and vomiting resulting from cancer chemotherapy. Several studies have produced evidence that it's effective in reducing spasticity-related pain and pain resulting from surgical procedures.[35]

Cannador (from the Society for Clinical Research, Germany) is used in Europe and contains a whole plant extract of cannabis. Clinical trials have shown it to be promising for relieving symptoms associated with multiple sclerosis, and for postoperative pain management.[36]

Perhaps the most promising botanically derived cannabis extract is a mouth spray called Nabiximols (brand name, Sativex) manufactured by a small research company, G. W. Pharmaceuticals, in Britain. Controlled studies done since 2004 revealed it to be effective in treating central neuropathic pain (resulting from nerve injury) and spasticity in multiple sclerosis, pain associated with rheumatoid arthritis, and pain in patients with advanced cancer. Already approved in twenty countries, including the United Kingdom, Spain, New Zealand, and Canada, Sativex, as of this writing, is still undergoing clinical studies in the United States as a prelude to FDA approval.[37]

Some decry Sativex and other medicinal forms of marijuana,

claiming that "Big Pharma" is unnecessarily inserting itself into the marijuana business, when individuals could be growing and distributing their own marijuana. While I most definitely sympathize with the argument that the pharmaceutical industry has at times been reckless and less than rigorous when it comes to safeguarding public health, I think that a regulated system of medication attempting to ensure, for example, the safety and efficacy of a drug, is important. All medications require strict certification of their ingredients, standardization of their products, and proper handling by medical professionals. This has gotten lost in the medical marijuana movement today.

In fact, we owe it to people who are truly sick, who are in legitimate pain, and who are dying, to characterize and standardize the medicine so it's properly labeled, so we know what's in it, so it's tested for mold and potency and additives by independent labs, and so it's dispensed by qualified medical personnel. People in need deserve access to medicine that we know is safe and effective.

MYTH

3

COUNTLESS PEOPLE ARE BEHIND BARS SIMPLY FOR SMOKING MARIJUANA

C riminal penalties for possessing small amounts of marijuana used to be quite severe in many US states. The cultural communication gap between marijuana users and public officials was also wide and deep.

As a revealing and somewhat humorous illustration, in 1970, the governor of Texas, Preston Smith, heard protestors chanting "Free Lee Otis, Free Lee Otis" during one of his speeches. Lee Otis Johnson was a black man serving thirty years in a Texas prison for giving one "joint" (a single cigarette) of marijuana to another person.

Governor Smith thought he heard the protestors chanting,

"Frijoles, Frijoles," and asked a reporter, "What do these people have against beans?"[1] Beyond the humor, this story came to symbolize both the racial profiling of drug law enforcement at that time and the deaf ear that public officials were turning to emerging public indignation toward the far-too-severe criminal penalties for marijuana.

Many of the earliest and most severe laws against marijuana were inspired by fear and racism. In the case of Texas, when its first law criminalizing marijuana possession was passed by the state legislature in 1919, a state senator and proponent of the law explained the rationale for passage this way: "All Mexicans are crazy, and this stuff [referring to marijuana] is what makes them crazy."[2] These early anti-marijuana sentiments in Texas seemed to spring from a fear that the migration of Mexicans into Texas would take jobs away from native state residents.

Between 1914 and 1931, beginning with the states of California and Utah, laws restricting the use and sale of marijuana were enacted in twenty-six states using a mix of misdemeanor and felony penalties. "From a survey of contemporary newspaper and periodical commentary," wrote the authors of a *Virginia Law Review* analysis of marijuana laws and their origin in 1970, "we have concluded… the most prominent [influence] was racial prejudice. During this period, marijuana legislation was generally a regional phenomenon present in the southern and western states. Use of the drug was primarily limited to Mexican-Americans who were immigrating in increased numbers to those states. These movements were well noted in the press accounts of passage of marijuana legislation."[3]

Lurid newspaper headlines stirred up by "yellow journalist" William Randolph Hearst and other newspaper owners spread the notion that marijuana was a "killer weed" because those high on it were likely to commit murder and other violent crimes. In Colorado, for instance, the *Denver Post* went on a campaign in 1929, to show that a Mexican man accused of killing a young girl did so because he "was a marijuana addict."[4]

Hollywood took note of this trend to demonize marijuana and, in response, a film company bankrolled by a church group released the notorious low-budget "exploitation circuit" movie, *Reefer Madness* in 1936 (the original title was *Tell Your Children*). The film is about a group of high school students who try marijuana for the first time and quickly become "dope fiends," descending into madness and engaging in manslaughter, suicide, and attempted rape.[5] The original theatrical release poster for the film screamed in bold lettering, "Women Cry For It—Men Die For It. Drug-Crazed Abandon."

Given the offensive sentiments and events that shaped the original laws regulating marijuana use, it's no wonder that in the 1960s, with the eruption and spread of youthful cynicism and mistrust of government, the pendulum of public opinion swung far the other way, generating many fevered myths about marijuana to inflame the public imagination.

THE MARIJUANA TREATMENT PENDULUM SWINGS WILDLY

By the 1950s, nearly every state had criminal penalties on the books for marijuana possession and sale. Federal penalties also increased as court decisions opened the way for greater federal government involvement in drug regulation.

Under the Boggs Act passed by Congress in 1951, marijuana was lumped together with narcotics for the first time with uniform penalties for violators. A first-possession offense could subject the offender to a jail sentence of two to five years and a fine of $2,000.[6]

States got on the bandwagon by passing "little Boggs Acts" with similar penalties for marijuana possession and sale. By 1953, at least twenty-seven states had implemented Boggs Act penalty structures. Several more states, in particular Ohio and Louisiana, enacted penalties "substantially more severe than those passed previously in any Jurisdiction," according to a *Virginia Law Review* article from 1970.[7] In the case of Louisiana, possession sentences ranged from a five-year minimum, without possibility of parole or probation, up to a ninety-nine-year sentence for any amount.

Still another escalation in sentencing severity occurred in 1956, with congressional approval of Public Law 728, known as the Narcotic Drugs Import and Export Act, which increased the fine to $20,000 and mandatory minimum sentences of two years for possession. Simple possession of any amount was, under the provisions of this law, considered sufficient evidence of guilt to automatically convict the defendant.[8]

Once again, states followed the federal escalation in penalties. One extreme example was Virginia, which in 1958, enacted a law making the possession of more than twenty-five grains of marijuana a crime punishable by imprisonment for not less than twenty years. Strangely, this penalty for possession was twice as severe as the penalty for unlawful sale of the drug.[9]

Marijuana possession was a felony with jail time in all states of the United States well into the 1960s, when a cultural shift occurred that rapidly changed attitudes and sentencing policies.

"When the youth counterculture emerged," commented a 2009 *CBS News* documentary on marijuana, "its embrace of drugs forced lawmakers and police to deal with a sudden demographic change. Marijuana was no longer a problem confined to Hispanics and blacks. The sons and daughters of the white middle class were also toking up, and in significant numbers."[10]

DECRIMINALIZATION BECOMES A NEW TREND

Public attitudes and law enforcement policies have undergone numerous changes of direction over the decades.

Congress abolished mandatory minimum sentencing at the federal level for marijuana and other drug offenses in 1970; states followed suit by lowering penalties for possessing small amounts of marijuana. During the 1970s, eleven states (starting with Oregon in 1973) decriminalized the use of small amounts of the plant, and many other states reduced the criminal penalties on use and possession.[11]

California was the first state to criminalize marijuana possession in the early twentieth century, and six decades later, in 1975, it was one of the states to drastically reduce criminal penalties on possession, making personal possession of an ounce or less a misdemeanor (instead of a felony) with a maximum fine of $100. In 2010, the penalty fell even more.[12] This decriminalizing trend accelerated until the late 1970s, and nearly thirty years later, voters in Massachusetts passed an initiative, in 2008, that decriminalized up to one ounce of marijuana, making possession a $100 civil fine.[13]

Cities also got into the decriminalization act, sometimes coming into conflict with state laws. Denver, Colorado, voters, for example, gave new meaning to the moniker "the Mile-High City" when they voted to make possession of up to an ounce of marijuana legal in 2005. A year later, the Denver City Council made arrests and ticketing for marijuana offenses the lowest priority for local law enforcement. Other cities, such as Seattle, Washington, and Oakland, California, did the same.[14]

There are a lot of unsubstantiated claims out there about marijuana and the criminal justice system:

"Unfortunately, the bulk of our nation's current anti-drug efforts and priorities remain fixated on arresting and jailing drug consumers—particularly recreational marijuana smokers."[15]

"We're also a nation overrun with robbers, rapists, murderers, wife beaters, child molesters. We say we're petrified of them. Yet we're releasing them first from overcrowded jails so dope smokers can take their cells."[16]

"Though there aren't enough cells for violent criminals, marijuana smokers and small-time dealers are going to prison by the thousands—sometimes for life."[17]

They are fear-based, hyperbolic statements, not data. The reality, according to studies by the Bureau of Justice, is that only *one-tenth of one percent* of people in state prisons are serving sentences for first-time marijuana possession. Just three-tenths of one percent of people in state prisons are serving time for marijuana possession if they have prior offenses, and only 1.4 percent of people are in jail for offenses involving only marijuana-related crimes.[18]

Most people arrested for marijuana possession in this country don't, in fact, end up in prison. Many of those who are charged for possession are pleading down from more serious charges, usually trafficking. Many marijuana arrests, as numerous studies have shown, "are incidental to traffic stops, drug enforcement more generally, disorderly conduct, and other enforcement activities."[19] In a situation where a driver is pulled over for speeding and the driver happens to be found with marijuana, marijuana would be the only arrest reported to the FBI, since it is more serious than speeding. This masks the fact that police would have taken action regardless of the marijuana.[20]

According to some leading drug policy researchers in the United States, the chance for arrest is one in every eleven thousand to twelve thousand joints smoked. The probability of being arrested during a year of monthly consumption rose to about 3 percent for adults and 6 percent for adolescents.[21] This isn't anti-marijuana propaganda. The latter two researchers, Peter Reuter and Rob MacCoun, have argued for relaxing today's marijuana laws for other reasons.[22]

Unless it is in the context of a parole or probation violation, virtually no one is serving prison time for using small amounts of marijuana. People indeed might spend some time in jail due to an arrest, but the statistics can be misleading. Consider this example: A person is pulled over for a broken taillight. When the police officer approaches the driver, he smells marijuana in the car. He also runs a background check (which he could have done regardless of the marijuana smell) and finds out that the driver is on probation and also wanted for a burglary earlier that week. The officer arrests the driver for the marijuana offense and the burglary. The driver gets two years for the burglary and for violating his terms of probation, and one-month concurrent for the marijuana charge. Technically, the driver is recorded as serving time for marijuana possession (as well as for burglary).

Few people in law enforcement want to throw everyone in prison for possessing small amounts of marijuana. Such an attitude was much more common thirty years ago, when penalties for marijuana possession in various states were generally much more severe.

Evidence published in peer-reviewed journals has shown that more than 85 percent of people serving prison time for all combined drug law violations were clearly involved in drug distribution, not just possession for personal use. Many of the remaining 15 percent answered questions suggesting possible involvement in drug distribution; the proportion of respondents serving time just for possession of amounts suitable for personal consumption was very small, perhaps on the order of 1 percent.[23]

In fact, researchers reported only about two-tenths of 1 percent of all prison inmates appeared to be incarcerated in prison simply for marijuana use. They analyzed data from the 1997 *Survey of Inmates in Federal and Correctional Facilities*[24] and found that the "number of marijuana users in prison [only] for their use is perhaps 800–2,300 individuals or on the order of 0.1–0.2 percent of all prison inmates"—numbers consistent with prior analysis released by the Office of National Drug Control Policy. Researchers estimated that the resulting expected time served in prison per *year* of use for marijuana was .04 days.[25]

Other federal data has shown that the median amount of marijuana for those convicted of marijuana possession is 115 pounds— or 156,000 marijuana cigarettes.[26]

Data on federal prisoners in 2011 from the US Sentencing Commission confirm that low-level users are not the targets of US prison policy:

- Of the 6,961 marijuana offenders in federal prison in 2011, only 103 of them were there for simple possession. The vast majority were there for drug trafficking and received no mandatory minimum sentence.[27]
- Federal marijuana offenders were the most likely of all drug offenders to receive a reduction in sentencing.[28]
- The government convicted only forty-eight federal marijuana offenders (possession and trafficking) having less than 5,000 grams of marijuana (the average was about 3,800 grams—about 8,000–10,000 joints).[29]

ARRESTS VERSUS JAILING

Just because people are generally not jailed for marijuana use—let alone marijuana sales—it doesn't mean that contact with the criminal justice system as a result of marijuana possession is rare. Indeed, according to FBI reports, law enforcement reported more than 800,000 arrests for marijuana possession last year. And that is a favorite statistic of the legalization camp—that we arrest hundreds of thousands of people every year and that it costs the judicial system tens of millions of dollars.

It is true that police make many arrests, but there are some serious and important caveats that need to be discussed. First and most importantly, most localities treat marijuana possession like a parking ticket. Most often someone is arrested, given a ticket, and asked to appear before a judge later and to pay a fine (the fine can sometimes cost less than the procedure to collect it!). That is why New York City made headlines in the 1990s, when Mayor Rudy Giuliani and Police Chief Bill Bratton made a conscious decision to target "low-level offenses" like unwanted squeegeeing, subway turnstile jumping, and smoking marijuana by arresting *and* detaining offenders.

Even given these caveats about arrests, I'll never forget what my former boss, Obama drug czar Gil Kerlikowske once told me: "When you get the cuffs on a kid, his life is forever changed, jail or not." I think that is a powerful statement, and I've reflected on it many times. There is no doubt that an arrest—even one not resulting in jail—is a powerful experience that can follow an individual for a long time in the form of a criminal record. That is why I advocate for laws that do not discriminate against those with records for small-time marijuana possession only—for instance, for getting college loans, public housing, or other benefits. We don't have good data on the number of people affected by a criminal record tarnished only with marijuana possession arrests, but the number is likely nontrivial.

I also believe that marijuana arrests disproportionally affect those from underprivileged socioeconomic groups, including racial minorities. An African-American or Latino youth smoking marijuana outdoors—in a public housing complex, for example—is surely more likely to get arrested than a white kid smoking indoors in his mom's basement. It is obvious that legalization would do little to counter the racial and socioeconomic factors at play here, but marijuana arrests that lead to a punitive sanction—rather than, for example, a health- or education-oriented intervention (as I will discuss in the afterword)—can be counterproductive. Indeed, by restricting future opportunities, we may inadvertently push people back into the illicit economy. That is not helpful for anyone.

WOULD ARRESTS GO *UP* UNDER LEGALIZATION?

No one really knows what would happen if we had widespread marijuana legalization. But if legal alcohol is any indication, under marijuana legalization we might have even *more* arrests and more police involvement with the drug than we do now. Legalization would mean more use, and thus more violations of marijuana-related regulations, more public intoxication violations, and an increased probability of drivers high on marijuana on the roads. To examine this argument in greater detail, I looked at the criminal justice costs of alcohol today.

To my surprise, I found that in 2009 alone, there were 2.7 million arrests for alcohol-related violations, *not* including violent crime. These 2.7 million arrests came from public drunkenness, the violation of liquor laws (like drinking-age limits), and driving while intoxicated.[30] In contrast, arrests for marijuana violations stand at *less than one-third* of alcohol arrests.

Indeed, our experience with alcohol indicates that laws and regulations around legal marijuana could result in *much higher costs* to the criminal justice system, in addition to increasing healthcare costs. This is a rarely discussed paradox.

Additionally, if alcohol and marijuana are used together, this compounds our problems. While it isn't a clear-cut case, the majority of studies investigating whether alcohol and marijuana are substitutes or complements suggest that the two drugs are used in a complementary way.[31] This is consistent with the literature on tobacco and marijuana, which suggests that they too are complements, not substitutes.[32,33]

Today in the United States there are about 15 million marijuana users compared to 129 million alcohol users and 70 million users of tobacco.[34] The legalization of marijuana will result in a huge expansion in the number of its users. And with this increase, comes an increase in its potential harms.

Keeping marijuana illegal—through the wise application of laws that do not stigmatize "youthful indiscretions," but instead focus on dealers—is as much a public safety policy as it is a public health policy.

ALTERNATIVES TO LONG-TERM INCARCERATION

How should we deal, then, with marijuana offenders without imposing harsh incarceration sentences? How do we get repeated low-level dealers, for example, to stop their behavior? The answer may be found in how we treat our own children.

When I was a kid, my mom would often ask me to clean my room. Most of the time, I did it with little fuss. But on those days when I was playing Nintendo or busy shooting hoops with friends, she would use modest and credible threats to get me to act—and they almost always worked. "Kevin," she would say, "if you don't clean up your room right now, you can't have friends over tonight and you can forget about going to that movie you wanted to see tomorrow. So get to work!" The immediacy and certainty of that threat got me every time. The godfather of public policy, Thomas Schelling, used to say that the best threat is the one that is *never carried out*. And my mom was a pro at making sure she never had to carry out her threats.

In my work with criminal populations, I have learned that criminals act like this too: they have poor impulse control; a propensity to attribute their misfortunes in life to either bad luck or actions beyond their own control; and a tendency to value immediate gratification, even if delaying gratification will result in a bigger eventual payoff. Psychologists and criminologists have long known that credible threats—usually swift, certain, but modest sanctions that occur close to the time of offense—are much more effective at behavior change than, say, severe threats carried out in the distant future (or not carried out at all).

Therefore it comes as no surprise that the largest segment of our criminal justice system—those in the community on probation or parole—often do not heed severe threats issued by the bench. Instead, they go on re-offending at the cost of billions of dollars to society. They are expected to change their behavior after hearing this from the judge—the criminal justice counterpart of "mom": "If you don't clean up your room right now, there is a 50 percent chance that in five months you will be grounded for six years!" These are the kinds of hollow threats that have produced a less-than-effective criminal justice system today.

That is why a once obscure program in Hawaii, aptly titled HOPE (Hawaii's Opportunity Probation with Enforcement), has received quite a bit of notice lately. This program has demonstrated remarkable success by simply employing swift, certain, and modest sanctions.[35] Tired of seeing the same offenders recidivating in his Hawaiian circuit court, Judge Steve Alm decided that he was going to start getting smart about sanctioning his probationers. Applying what we know about deterrence, he started issuing immediate but modest sanctions *every time* one of his probationers reoffended.

Beginning with a formal warning hearing, Judge Alm openly explains to his probationers that continued violations won't be tolerated and that each violation will result in an immediate jail stay. To track their behavior, offenders are assigned a color and must call in every morning to hear if their color is mentioned by the automated system. If it is, they must report at once for a drug test; no-shows are treated as positives and a warrant is immediately issued. Reoffenders appear before Judge Alm within one or two days and are offered treatment first. If they refuse, they immediately spend the next two days (not years or decades) in jail (weekends for employed probationers). After they serve their time, they continue in the program, with sanctions slowly escalating (repeat offenders are referred to a drug court or other treatment option).

Skeptics worried that without mandating treatment for all probationers at the start, many would reoffend and take up drugs again. Others were concerned that the jail population would sky-rocket—now that *the law was actually being carried out* for once. What resulted was nothing short of revolutionary. HOPE shattered myths about sentence length, drug use behavior, and the ability of the offender *and* public administrators to change their ways.

In a randomly controlled trial, HOPE far outperformed traditional probation.[36] Missed appointments and positive drug tests fell by over 80 percent. Jail stays decreased, and real dollars were saved. The traditional probation group—surprise—found no improvement in drug use, and their percentage of missed appointments actually increased. HOPE probationers viewed their sentences as fair, crime fell (arrests for new crimes were cut in half), and, best of all, people's lives turned around. Additionally, scarce treatment slots were reserved for those with the most serious addictions (i.e., those who could not stop their addiction through HOPE). A one-year randomized control experiment confirmed these results (see table 1, borrowed from the National Institute of Justice evaluation).

While applying HOPE principles to probation programs around

*Table 1. Probationer Outcomes during the One-Year Follow-up Period**

	Hope	*Control*
No-shows for probation appointments	9%	23%
Positive Urine Tests	13%	46%
New Arrest Rate	21%	47%
Probation Revocation Rate	7%	15%
Incarceration (Days Sentenced)	138 days	267 days

*Results are from the one-year randomized controlled trial portion of the evaluation.

the country is new (although HOPE-type programs are now present in many states around the US), the underpinnings of the program are well established. The first director of the NIDA, Dr. Robert L. DuPont, utilized similar strategies with resounding success among a population of drug-using physicians through the *Physician Health Program*.[37]

This program provides a safe place for addicted doctors to get treated (physicians have a high addiction rate among all professionals, partly due to easy access to powerful drugs). In return for participation in the program and the right to keep their job, physicians sign contracts, typically for five years, stipulating that they will adhere to the guidelines of the program. This includes entering treatment and agreeing to be randomly tested for drugs and alcohol. Physicians Health Programs have been in existence for more than 40 years, having started with the help of the American Medical Association. Another similar program, the 24/7 Sobriety program in South Dakota, ensures that people arrested for or convicted of alcohol-related offenses must abstain from alcohol (and to a lesser extend, drug use) in an effort to prevent future offending. The project utilizes twice-daily breath testing, transdermal alcohol monitoring ankle bracelets, urinalysis, and drug test patches to ensure compliance in a similar way to HOPE. Researchers from the think-tank RAND found a 12 percent reduction in repeat driving while intoxicated arrests on the county level, a 9 percent reduction of domestic violence arrests on the county level, and evidence suggested modest reductions in traffic crashes among male drivers eighteen to forty, the population most likely to participate in the program. RAND is in the process of undertaking a cost-benefit analysis of the program, but these initial results are encouraging.[38]

Additionally, thousands of drug courts across the country are predicated on swift and certain sanctions combined with treatment, and have been extremely successful in reducing drug use and reshaping lives and communities for the better. Since their inception at the state and local level in 1989, the number of drug courts has expanded, with more than two-thousand operating today. Generally, these types of courts offer marijuana offenders the option of avoiding any jail time if they agree to take part in a treatment program, submit to regular drug screenings, and report to a drug court judge for one year. If and when they complete the drug court program, those charges originally brought against them are either dropped, wiping their records clean, or the charges are reduced. Drug courts significantly reduce drug use and crime, and are more cost-effective than any other proven criminal justice strategy evaluated in the literature today.[39]

These kinds of interventions—drug courts, HOPE probation, 24/7 Sobriety, etc.—succeed because of the support they offer to the individual, the positive interaction they produce between judge and defendant, and the credible monitoring system they ensure.

But why aren't these methods implemented more often? It turns out that it is tough to change the old habits of the system. As Adele Herrell said after an evaluation of a drug court, "Changing addict behavior is easy. Changing judge behavior is hard."[40]

Smarter strategies targeting low-level street dealers have also emerged. One such program is called the Drug Market Initiative (DMI). Rather than arresting low-level dealers and putting them in jail, this program brings them to a community meeting where they meet with their parents, clergy, and neighbors.

This is how it works. Police use investigative techniques to make prosecutable cases against every drug dealer, and then arrest the volume sellers, violent offenders, and those facing probation, parole revocation hearings, or upcoming court dates. Law enforcement confronts the remaining people—the low-level dealers—with the "banked" prosecutable case against them. Low-level dealers who continue their behavior are put on notice that they will be arrested immediately without further investigation, but those who agree to stop participate in the "call-in." At a "call-in," these low-level offenders are confronted by community leaders, family, and law enforcement, people who voice intolerance for their criminal behavior and demand an end to their destructive actions.

If the offender agrees to straighten up, he or she is provided assistance in locating employment, housing, transportation, health care, and social services to help with their transition to a crime- and drug-free lifestyle. DMI is implemented one neighborhood at a time. Once drug dealing and violence are reduced in one target area, the team can select another area, and the process repeats.

Generally, it takes anywhere from seven to eleven months for a target neighborhood to reach the "call-in." In 2004, the original DMI in High Point, North Carolina, effectively reduced violent crime in the targeted neighborhood by 57 percent. DMI was then implemented elsewhere in High Point, eventually leading to the elimination of overt drug markets citywide. Recidivism among participating dealers dropped to half the state average.[41] High Point's success led to DMI implementation in cities across the country. After implementation in Providence, Rhode Island, calls for police service were down 58 percent, and reported drug crime dropped 70 percent. Nashville,

Tennessee, experienced a 23 percent decline in violent crime and a 49 percent decline in narcotics violations following DMI implementation.[42] Residents of DMI communities report substantial improvements in the quality of their lives. Furthermore, neighborhoods surrounding the targeted areas have also experienced significant declines in crime, implying that there was no displacement of crime.

Such innovative criminal justice solutions grounded in sound research enhance prevention, treatment, and enforcement without resorting to severe penalties. These approaches recognize that swiftness and certainty of punishment can be a key to changing unhealthy behaviors.

Our criminal justice system is vital to the public health of Americans, which is why we must use that system wisely. Our only two options aren't legalization and long-term incarceration. There are many other strategies (I've only highlighted a few here) that can be implemented with success.

By using both incentives and coercion where necessary, and doing so wisely, our criminal justice system can advance the cause of public health and public safety.

MYTH 4

THE LEGALITY OF ALCOHOL AND TOBACCO STRENGTHEN THE CASE FOR LEGAL MARIJUANA

"What's the big deal?" is the attitude of a lot of people toward marijuana today. "Alcohol and tobacco are worse for you, and they are legal," goes the reasoning, "so pot should be legal too. We should be consistent, right?" In fact, as I argue here, our experience with alcohol and tobacco provide a clear warning *against* legalization.

Alcohol kills one-hundred-thousand people annually. Tobacco kills another five hundred thousand people every year. Our two legal drugs are the biggest contributors to healthcare costs in this country. In many respects, because of its prevalence, alcohol is far worse than *any* of our currently illegal drugs, including crack. For example, alcohol causes much more violence and murder in our society than any other drug.

So I have little faith that we would handle legal marijuana—or any other legalized drug for that matter—much better. Indeed, modeling marijuana on alcohol and tobacco policy is a risky proposition for many reasons.

As I've argued earlier, one can be *against* marijuana legalization while wholeheartedly agreeing that our current policies can be greatly improved. We can do a whole lot better (and I talk more about this in the afterword). But legalization won't solve most of our problems and will, in fact, create a host of new and more intractable ones. Alcohol and tobacco—our two legal drugs—are prime examples of substances burdening society with both obvious and subtle consequences. The costs of these drugs to society greatly overshadow any gains derived from their taxation.

To begin, the total social costs associated with our legal drugs—roughly $200 billion per substance—far outweigh any tax revenue we collect from their use. In fact, these costs—from healthcare expenditures due to alcohol and tobacco use, to lost productivity, to accidents—are *ten times greater than any tax revenue federal and state governments receive* from the taxation of these two legalized drugs.[1] That's right. For every dollar in tax revenue we get from alcohol and tobacco sales, we lose $10 in social costs.

The public health toll of our legal drugs is enormous. These drugs are pushed by big corporations with no incentive to curb use.

Indeed, one only needs to peek at the commercial playbook of the tobacco industry to get a sense of what could happen under marijuana legalization.

BIG TOBACCO WILL MORPH INTO BIG CANNABIS

Do we really want Big Cannabis to emerge and become like Big Tobacco, making lots of money from people's addictions and burdening society with perpetually increasing healthcare costs?

Under legalization, we can expect big businesses to emerge and commercialize marijuana. Some of those businesses could conceivably be the same Big Tobacco companies that have spent more than a century selling tobacco cigarettes. Tobacco company business plans may already be taking this eventuality into account. In 1970, Brown and Williamson, now merged with R.J. Reynolds, had a consultant look into the prospect of getting into the marijuana business:

> The use of marijuana...has important implications for the tobacco industry in terms of an alternative product line. [We] have the land to grow it, the machines to roll it and

package it, the distribution to market it. In fact, some firms have registered trademarks, which are taken directly from marijuana street jargon. These trade names are used currently on little-known legal products, but could be switched if and when marijuana is legalized. Estimates indicate that the market in legalized marijuana might be as high as $10 billion annually.[2]

Fast forward to 2012 and Altria, the new name of tobacco giant Philip Morris, had this to say when asked if they had plans to get into the marijuana business: "We never speculate on what our future plans may or may not be."[3] This is from the same company that recently bought the domain names "AltriaCannabis.com" and "AltriaMarijuana.com," reportedly to protect them from other groups misusing their brand.

An analysis conducted at the University of Nevada Business School examined whether the tobacco manufacturer Phillip Morris is "a good fit for Mary Jane," and went on to conclude: "Phillip Morris could be very successful at making marijuana profitable."[4]

The business analysis noted that the "most likely regulation of the industry would be in the form of licensing to different firms for the production and distribution of the product. Expensive licenses would be granted to the firms that have prior experience in similar industries, like tobacco or alcohol...only a few firms could handle this responsibility."

Because a company like Phillip Morris is already involved in the manufacture and sale of both tobacco and alcohol, along with its food services branch of operation, it would be strategically placed to create "synergies" of complementing products. For instance, the University of Nevada analysis noted how "complements could range from free snack foods with the purchase of marijuana to 'buy a 12-pack of Icehouse [beer], get one pack of Marlboro Greens free.' By creating synergies for buyers more value will be given, and higher profits will be achieved."

And in 2013, with much fanfare, and alongside the ex-President of Mexico Vicente Fox, former head of Microsoft corporate strategy James Shivley announced that he was creating "the Starbucks of marijuana." His plan? To buy up medical marijuana dispensaries in Colorado and Washington state, "mint[ing] more millionaires than Microsoft in this business." At the end of his news conference, he said "Let's go big or go home."[5]

For insight into how "Big Marijuana" might interact with its pool of potential customers, we have only to examine the tobacco industry's history of interactions with the public and with various regulatory agencies. Here is how that record of deception and manipulation was described in a 2010 federal court document prepared by a national network of legal centers, the Tobacco Control Legal Consortium:

> For more than half a century, tobacco companies have en-
> gaged in an unrelenting campaign to deceive the American
> public and the United States government about the health
> effects of their deadly products. The companies have denied
> the lethal effects of smoking, of secondhand smoke, and of
> smokeless tobacco use. They have targeted their advertising
> at youth to replenish the supply of smokers and manipulated
> the levels of nicotine in their products to ensure that users

remain addicted. And through it all they cynically offered a series of allegedly less harmful innovations—from filters to "light" cigarettes to new "smokeless" products—that in fact, when used, were no safer at all, but that dissuaded smokers from ending their use of tobacco. The campaign of deception has involved the suppression of scientific evidence, the hiding and destruction of documents, and the enlistment of supposedly objective research institutions and scientific experts paid by tobacco companies to sow doubt and confusion.[6]

Publicly, Big Tobacco was very clear that their marketing efforts were never meant to hook kids. For decades, they publicly declared that children and youths were not targeted:[7]

"[O]ur Company welcomes the opportunity to make it clear that we do not promote the sale of tobacco products to children." (American Tobacco Co.)

"We are not for getting youth to smoke, I want to make that plain right now." (Congressional testimony of Bowman Gray, Chairman of the Board of R.J. Reynolds on behalf of the entire industry)

"[W]e segment the market, and the segmentation we use in our marketing to develop marketing strategies, I will make the point very clearly here that not one of those segments, and there are many, is the youth segment." (Congressional testimony of Ed Horrigan, R.J. Reynolds)

"In our view, smoking is an adult custom and the decision to smoke should be based on mature and informed individual freedom of choice." (1993 Tobacco Institute press release)

"We Don't Advertise to Children." (R.J. Reynolds advertisement, 1994)

"Minors should not smoke. Period. That is our position." (Philip Morris advertisement)

Sounds good, right? In fact it sounds a lot like current businesses today that have emerged in light of recent medical marijuana and legalization laws in the United States. Well, secret documents obtained during the landmark Tobacco Master Settlement Agreement of 1998—which forced tobacco companies to disclose their practice—show that the tobacco companies were engaging in nothing less than willful deceit:[8]

"[T]he base of our business is the high school student." (Secret Documents obtained from Lorillard after the Tobacco Master Settlement Agreement of 1998)

"[W]e must get our share of the youth market....The fragile, developing self-image of the young person needs all of the support and enhancement it can get. Smoking may appear to enhance that self-image....Psychologically, at eighteen one is immortal....In this sense, the warning label...may be a plus." (Secret Documents obtained from R.J. Reynolds after the Tobacco Master Settlement Agreement of 1998)

"[T]he 14-18 year old group is an increasing segment.... RJR must soon establish a successful new brand in this market if our position in the industry is to be maintained over the long-term." (Secret Documents obtained from R.J. Reynolds after the Tobacco Master Settlement Agreement of 1998)

"[Young people are] the only source of replacement smokers...."(Secret Documents obtained from R.J. Reynolds after the Tobacco Master Settlement Agreement of 1998)

"It is important to know as much as possible about teenage smoking patterns and attitudes. Today's teenager is tomorrow's potential regular customer, and the overwhelming majority of smokers first begin to smoke while still in their teens...." (Secret Documents obtained from R.J. Reynolds after the Tobacco Master Settlement Agreement of 1998)

"[In] an attempt to reach young smokers, starters should be based, among others, on the following major parameters: Present the cigarette as one of a few initiations into the adult world.... Don't communicate health or health-related points." (Secret Documents obtained from Brown and Williamson after the Tobacco Master Settlement Agreement of 1998)

"You may recall that two years ago I wrote a memo and gave talks at a Richmond meeting and in New York on trends in smoking prevalence among high school seniors and college freshmen. At that time smoking prevalence was declining at an increasing rate, and that fact, plus the decline in the absolute number of people reaching 18, did not auger well for future cigarette sales. I have just received data on the graduation class of 1982 [high school] and the results are much more encouraging...."(Secret Documents obtained from Phillip Morris after the Tobacco Master Settlement Agreement of 1998)

"[I]n this study, no lower age limit was set...with the intentions of probing the dynamics of the market...as a guide for future direction." (Secret Documents obtained from Phillip Morris after the Tobacco Master Settlement Agreement of 1998)

"The most important finding, and the one of the greatest significance to the company, is...price elasticity of cigarettes among teenagers....[A] ten percent increase in price would lead to a 14 percent decline in cigarette consumption by teenagers....We can never look with equanimity on increases in excise tax..." (Secret Documents obtained from Phillip Morris after the Tobacco Master Settlement Agreement of 1998)

Furthermore, as I will show happens with the liquor industry today, we know that Big Tobacco targeted the poor and communities of color. When the "Winston Man," model Dave Goerlitz, finished with a photo session for R.J. Reynolds one day, he asked the executives present if he could take home some props—a few cartons of cigarettes. He was surprised when the executives replied that they did not smoke. "Are you kidding?" one of the executives said. "*We reserve that right for the poor, the young, the black, and the stupid.*"[9] Goerlitz, who was severely disabled by a stroke due to his tobacco use, now counsels kids on why smoking is dangerous.

Is there any reason to believe that, with huge profits looming and free commercial speech in the United States, the same patterns won't follow the emergence of a legal marijuana industry? I doubt it. The seeds of this chicanery have already been sown. We can see it on display right now with the tactics and rhetoric being used by the

A mid-century advertisement for Camel cigarettes. Tobacco companies paid lavish sums to the medical industry in return for endorsements. (from the collection of Standord University, tobacco.stanford.edu)

pro-legalization groups. Indeed, many of the same arguments the marijuana legalization folks have made—like smoked marijuana is medicine—were claimed by Big Tobacco a half–century ago.

Here are more claims often made, found on websites through a simple google search. *"Marijuana cures cancer. Marijuana could not be safer. Marijuana is God's herb. Legal marijuana will solve Mexico's violence problem. Marijuana Prohibition is making career criminals out of ordinary folks."* The mythmaking goes on and on.

THE LIQUOR LOBBY

It is well established that alcohol manufacturers do not make money off the casual drinker. They make their profits from the heavy user— the person who has five drinks a day, not the one drink a week.[10] And heavy drinkers become heavy drinkers because they start early, so alcohol manufacturers have every incentive to target youths.[11]

This point was elucidated by Mark Kleiman, Professor of Public Policy at the UCLA Luskin School of Public Affairs and editor of the *Journal of Drug Policy Analysis.* Professor Kleiman, who has been equally skeptical of anti-marijuana efforts and the marijuana legalization movement, commented: "The entire marketing effort [for alcohol] is devoted to cultivating and maintaining the people whose use is a problem to them and a gold mine to the industry.…Divide the population into deciles by annual drinking volume. The top decile starts at four drinks a day, averaged year-round. That group consumes half of all the alcohol sold.…[The] booze companies cannot afford to have their customers 'drink in moderation'.…[Most] of those folks [heavy drinkers] have an alcohol abuse disorder. And they're the target market....[So] the prospect of a legal cannabis industry working hard to produce as many chronic stoners as possible, and fighting hard against any sort of effective regulation, fills me with fear."[12]

Does all of this mean that I think alcohol should be prohibited? My answer (to some people's surprise) is no. Alcohol has a very particular cultural history and enjoys a unique cultural status in our current society—a level of widespread cultural acceptance and use (think of champagne toasts at weddings or the role of wine in the Bible) that marijuana does not have. While I personally don't drink, I respect our current laws around alcohol legalization and believe that, given current conditions, their reversal would be a public policy disaster. Many public health professionals I talk to call the legalization of alcohol a *cultural accident* because if we were considering public health and safety outcomes alone, alcohol would not be a drug to legalize. But alcohol, unlike marijuana and other drugs, has a long history of widespread use in our culture. Marijuana has had only limited public acceptance at different times in our history.

There is a deep US history with alcohol. And for better or for worse, we're stuck with it. That doesn't mean we can't make alcohol policy better. We can. We know, for example, that while alcohol taxes won't come close to covering the social costs of the drug, raising them would help to reduce consumption rates and the health problems associated with heavy drinking. [13,14] To paraphrase Kleiman, "Any sentence about illegal drug policy that does not have 'raise alcohol taxes' at the end of it is an incoherent sentence." We could also do a better job of regulating liquor outlets and limiting advertising. But all of these policy measures are difficult to implement because there is a powerful, rich legal alcohol industry lobbying for policies beneficial to their bottom line.

Anyone who knows anything about the alcohol business cannot help but chuckle when Super Bowl television beer ads tell us to "enjoy responsibly." If everyone *did* enjoy responsibly, the alcohol industry would be out of business. Drinking responsibly is not part of their business plan. Why would a legal marijuana industry be any different?

The Supreme Court ruled 6–3 in 2011(*Sorrell* v. *IMS Health*) that *commercial speech is free speech*. It's therefore a very safe bet that if marijuana is legalized, marijuana advertising will flourish. There used to be a voluntary alcohol industry limit on advertising hard liquor. Not anymore. The alcohol industry now advertises vodka and other hard liquors with abandon. We cannot rely on an addictive industry to police its own; there's no incentive. In fact, in Colorado, advertising limits recommended by the state task force charged with advising the governor on implementing marijuana legalization are now being challenged by the marijuana industry. And this promises to be only the beginning.

Do you ever wonder why liquor stores tend to be located more densely in poor neighborhoods than in well-to-do suburbs? (Studies have consistently shown that alcohol is far more available in neighborhoods with communities of color versus white neighborhoods.[15]) Why are lottery dispensers easily found in the economically depressed areas of East Los Angeles but rarely seen in Beverly Hills? The reason is that these addictive industries target the most vulnerable. Addicts in Compton have a harder time writing a $50,000 check to the Betty Ford Treatment Center than people in Beverly Hills. Marijuana legalization would widen the gap between the rich and poor even more.

ALCOHOL PROHIBITION CONTINUES TO GENERATE LESSONS

It is commonly accepted that Alcohol Prohibition was a failure in this country because it was a widely ignored ban that created a black market in sales, which, in turn, enriched criminal syndicates. We've all heard the stories about bathtub gin killing hundreds of people.

But was there an upside to Prohibition? A professor of criminal justice at Harvard's Kennedy School of Government, Mark H. Moore, investigated that question and came up with some interesting data, shedding new light on what we think we know about that period in American history.[16]

Here are a few of his findings:

- Alcohol consumption did decline significantly during Prohibition, one indication being that the rate of cirrhosis deaths for men, which had been 29.5 per 100,000 men before Prohibition, fell to just 10.7 deaths per 100,000 during the ban.
- State mental hospital admissions for alcoholic psychosis also underwent a dramatic decline, falling from 10.1 per 100,000 persons to less than 5 at the height of Prohibition.
- Arrests for disorderly conduct and public drunkenness fell by half.

The prohibition of alcohol in the United States became law in 1920, and was repealed at the federal level in 1933, though the alcohol ban continued in some localities around the nation, and remains in place in a few counties of Texas, Louisiana, and Mississippi even up to the present day.

MYTH 4

A relatively recent example of Prohibition comes from the northernmost city in the United States, Barrow, Alaska. Fed up with the crime that open alcohol use was causing, residents voted to ban alcohol within the city limits in 1994. The results were dramatic. During the period that the alcohol ban was in effect (pro-alcohol residents summoned enough support to repeal it a year later), the following occurred:

- Crime decreased 70 percent within the city.
- Alcohol-related emergency room visits went from 123 the month before the ban to only 23 the next month.
- Once the ban was lifted and alcohol became available in the city again, local detoxification centers filled with patients and alcohol-related murders were on the rise again.[17]

Barrow's experience represents a microcosm of what happened nationwide during the fourteen years that Prohibition was in effect throughout the United States: public health improved.

As I mentioned earlier, for a whole host of cultural factors, all of this is not a reason to bring back Alcohol Prohibition. But it does show that when a drug is illegal, public health improves since the drug is neither as commercialized nor as normalized as it would be if it was legal.

WOULD CARTELS AND VIOLENCE DISAPPEAR UNDER MARIJUANA LEGALIZATION?

One commonly made argument is that marijuana legalization would destroy—or at least substantially cripple—organized crime and criminal organizations, like the bloody Mexican cartels. But anyone familiar with US history knows that organized crime flourished even after Prohibition was ended.

When Alcohol Prohibition expressly handed over alcohol policy to state governments (and thus essentially ended the practice in most places) in 1933, organized crime syndicates families made up the income lost from illegal bootlegging by expanding into gambling, prostitution, illegal drugs, and labor racketeering. These criminal gangs had always been involved in multiple vices, so the loss of revenue from illegal alcohol sales was just a short-term blow to their livelihoods.

To examine whether the Mexican drug cartels would undergo a similar shift in activities if marijuana was legalized, a team of researchers from the RAND Drug Policy Research Center conducted a thorough study of the subject in 2010. Their analysis remains the most comprehensive examination of the Mexican drug trafficking organizations, the violence they instigate, and their capabilities to expand beyond the marijuana market.

Almost every day, we see heartbreaking news headlines about the drug-related violence in Mexico, particularly along the US border. Nearly ten thousand people a year are being murdered in the carnage. Both Presidents George W. Bush and Barack Obama voiced the belief that America's drug consumption was the root cause of this horrific and destabilizing violence.[18]

When the Proposition 19 marijuana legalization initiative was on the ballot in California in 2010, proponents argued that "marijuana prohibition has created vicious drug cartels across our border," and that legalization would "cut off funding to violent drug cartels across our border who currently generate 60 percent of their revenues from the illegal US marijuana market."[19] (The 60 percent figure was obtained from a 2004 estimate by the Office of National Drug Control Policy but disavowed in 2010.)

As the RAND research team scrutinized this argument, they discovered that marijuana exports are an important but not dominant source of revenue for Mexican drug cartels. RAND estimated that "15–26 percent is a more credible range of the share of drug export revenues attributable to marijuana" at that time.[20] That works out to around $1.5 billion in cartel revenues coming from moving marijuana across the US border for sale to wholesalers. By contrast, cocaine, heroin, and methamphetamine trafficking into the United States brought the cartels over $5 billion a year in revenues (combined total, not per drug).[21] Consistent with this finding, the Mexican Institute of Competitiveness (IMCO), found that Mexican drug cartels could see their revenue drop between 20 and 33 percent. The lead author wrote later that he thought "that could be reasonably termed both significant and substantial...[however] marijuana legalization would transform the Mexican drug trafficking organizations (in interesting and, as of yet, unpredictable ways), but it would certainly not eliminate them (not by itself, in any case)."[22]

Where do the cartels derive most of their income if not from marijuana trafficking? They traffic cocaine, heroin, and methamphetamine into the United States. They smuggle migrants across the border (and when migrants refuse to cooperate in cartel activities, they are often murdered, sometimes in mass killings, dozens at a time). These crime syndicates profit from extortion and kidnapping. They traffic in weapons and ammunition. In short, like the crime syndicates during Alcohol

Prohibition, the Mexican cartels have "diversified their portfolio" and spread their tentacles into a wide range of vices, and these activities have further jacked up levels of violence as the various cartels compete to control turf.[23]

Legalizing marijuana is clearly not a panacea for reducing the influence of Mexican crime syndicates or their bloodthirsty cycle of violence.

LEGAL ALCOHOL AND TOBACCO SHOULD GIVE US PAUSE

Our long-term social experiments with alcohol and tobacco illustrate how an open market spreads greater harms. Legalization does not curb violence; it increases public health harms. Both alcohol and tobacco are relatively cheap and easy to obtain, as marijuana would be under legalization. Commercialization has glamorized their use and entrenched levels of social acceptance. The nature of addiction and the lure of enormous profits have led to unbridled marketing tactics. Addiction has simply become a price of doing business.

The legalization of marijuana would be a simplistic solution to a complicated problem. It would increase use and, with it, a host of attendant social problems. If anything, our experience with alcohol and tobacco over the past few centuries demonstrates that if these drugs are to be "models" for legal marijuana, then we'd better buckle our fiscal and psychological seatbelts, because we are in a for a long and rough ride.

MYTH

5

LEGAL MARIJUANA WILL SOLVE THE GOVERNMENT'S BUDGETARY PROBLEMS

"Legalize and tax it" has become a mantra of the pro-marijuana movement. It has proven to be a seductive message and a clever long-term strategy for making legalization more palatable to people who might not otherwise be inclined to tolerate drugs and drug use.

The tempting idea that taxing marijuana can raise significant new revenues strikes a responsive chord.

One major reason why Alcohol Prohibition was repealed was that repealers promised that alcohol taxes would make a federal income tax unnecessary, as Daniel Okrent reported in his brilliant book, *Last Call*.[1] But is that a realistic expectation? Will sufficient revenue be raised to offset the costs of the harms inflicted on individuals and society from wider marijuana use?

When President Barack Obama was questioned in 2011, about whether he believed that taxing legal marijuana would help relieve the nation's financial situation, he responded, "No, I don't think that is a good strategy to grow our economy."[2] His response was firmly grounded in the findings of many academic studies over the previous decade.

The social costs of marijuana production and use will far exceed what state and local governments collect as actual tax revenue. We've been down this road with alcohol. We've seen this pattern before. Society gains about $15 to $20 billion a year from the taxes imposed on alcohol, while it *loses* over $200 billion a year in healthcare, criminal justice, and other costs directly related to alcohol use and abuse. That's a ratio of 10 to 1 (or higher) of costs to revenue. Tobacco is hardly better. The $25 billion collected in tobacco taxes doesn't even come close to offsetting the more than $200 billion in lost social costs from tobacco use.

These sorts of trade-offs don't benefit taxpayers or institutions of government, and they certainly don't support the health needs of people unable to control their compulsion to abuse "sin taxed" substances as these become more widely available and socially accepted.

Taxing legal marijuana won't generate anywhere near the amount of government revenue that the pro-marijuana movement claims. At least five points support this contention.

FIVE WAYS TAX REVENUE ESTIMATES ARE UNREALISTIC

1. *Legalization Would Drive Marijuana Prices Down*

If marijuana is legalized using models adopted by Colorado and Washington, we will see the market price of marijuana fall considerably, but this drop in price is not factored into estimates of marijuana-generated tax revenue. According to RAND Corporation economist Rosalie Pacula's testimony before a committee of the California legislature, marijuana prices will fall to less than half the figure often employed in revenue estimates by some government budget analysts (some more recent analyses take into account this price drop, but not consistently).[3]

In 2010, when a team of five RAND researchers analyzed California's 2010 effort to legalize marijuana, they concluded that the pre-tax price of the drug could plummet (as much as 80 percent) and therefore marijuana consumption could increase.[4] This was based on a scenario where the federal government did not intervene and indoor home-production would be allowed.

That sharp drop in price complicates any attempts to predict the actual revenues that will result from marijuana taxes. Furthermore, the fall in price will hinder efforts to collect those revenues as a black market springs up to take advantage of the gap between the taxed price of marijuana and the real production cost of marijuana.

When legislation that would have legalized marijuana was introduced in the California legislature in 2010, the proposed tax would have been $50 an ounce paid at the point of retail, which equals $800 a pound. There would have also been a sales tax. Such a taxing structure would have created a huge incentive for home growers to undercut the state-sanctioned, state-taxed price per pound *and avoid paying taxes altogether.*

If a pound of marijuana can be produced for $75 or less, but in the legal market, the tax alone is at least $800 per pound, one can easily imagine how this discrepancy might cause many producers to stay in the black market to undercut the taxed legal price. This huge gap in costs would also cause consumers to seek out the lower-priced black market marijuana whenever and wherever possible.

Additionally, the other regulations that come with marijuana legalization will further strengthen the incentive for black market marijuana cultivation. If governments attempt to regulate the potency of state-sanctioned marijuana (i.e., to legally keep THC potency below a certain level), we can expect an underground market to furnish the higher-potency product that users seek. We can expect the underground market to flourish, which is not such a stretch when you look at the fact that illegal gambling has filled the gaps where legal gambling has fallen short (e.g., illegal gambling formats such as poker rooms and sports bookmaking flourish because their legal counterparts are unable or unwilling to provide the same services or betting options).[5]

2. *Lower Prices Increase Use and Harm*

As with any commodity, higher prices are associated with lower demand. That's a simple rule of economics. And it's especially the case with marijuana, because so much of the demand for the drug comes from teenagers and college students who are generally more limited in their incomes and access to financial resources. Given marijuana's costly harms to society—healthcare costs, car crashes, and so forth—an increase in use rates corresponds directly to an increase in the attendant social harms of the drug. In other words, lower prices mean greater harm.

It has been estimated that for every 10 percent reduction in the price of marijuana, there is a corresponding 3 percent increase in the number of users and a 5 percent increase in total quantity consumed, though it is impossible to know where those numbers "top out"—this depends on many factors.[6] As the price for an ounce of marijuana falls under legalized marijuana in the US, we can possibly expect hundreds of thousands of new users to enter the marketplace for marijuana, while thousands of current users increase their usage levels. Taxes can, of course, off-set this price collapse, but then high taxes could well invite gray and black markets to thrive.

Holland's experience with cannabis coffee shops provides an instructive example in this respect. After most legal penalties were removed from private possession and marijuana became more widely available through cannabis shops, usage doubled among young adults.[7]

In the United States, a 50 percent jump in the number of users would be substantial, with a ripple effect of repercussions.

Again, taking the example of California as a model for the nation, that state has already seen a gigantic escalation in the number of marijuana users seeking treatment for marijuana abuse or dependence. Between 1992 and 2008, there was a near quintupling of the number of treatment admissions due to marijuana, from seven thousand three hundred to nearly thirty-five thousand, far in excess of the admission numbers for other illicit drugs.[8] One explanation for the admissions upsurge is that THC potency intensified during that time frame, a situation that can only get worse under legalization as growers compete to offer more unique highs from their marijuana products.

3. Tax Revenues Would Be Exceeded by Harm Costs

Legalization would cost taxpayers a lot of money. There will be regulatory costs, legal costs, criminal justice and healthcare costs, a loss of productivity resulting from higher use, and so forth. These costs are rarely balanced adequately against the claim that marijuana will generate tax revenue.

RAND economist Rosalie Pacula testified before a committee of the California State Assembly in 2009: "As an economist who has been conducting drug policy analyses for almost 15 years, it is very important to consider a full cost-benefit analysis before undertaking large reforms like marijuana legalization." She pointed out numerous instances where the largely unrecognized costs of legalization would weigh heavily on society.[9]

For example, researchers studied hospital admissions for people with marijuana dependence as a primary diagnosis and determined that their "median lengths of stay are twice to three times longer than those experienced by patients admitted for alcohol, cocaine or heroin and therefore result in higher average charges."[10] For the uninsured, that means taxpayers are often called upon to pay for these costs through Medicaid and other health support programs.

Under any marijuana legalization scheme there will still be

criminal justice costs because there are expenses associated with regulating the industry. As I stated under the third myth, we already have almost 2.5 million arrests a year because of drunk driving violations, liquor law violations, and public intoxication. By contrast, marijuana-related arrests today stand at around eight hundred thousand.

4. Regulation and Tax Collection Costs Would Be High

Enforcing the regulatory and taxing provisions of a legalization law will require an expenditure of public resources. That much is certain. How much in the way of tax dollars will be needed remains a guesstimate depending on a wide variety of factors.

As with alcohol and the alcohol beverage boards created by most states as regulatory authorities, there would be a need for the creation of marijuana regulation enforcement bureaucracies at the state level. There would be changes in state and local government expenditures on law enforcement and drug treatment. Quality and safety control bureaucracies composed of health inspectors would have to be expanded, especially for inspecting facilities that produce baked goods containing marijuana. And agencies would have to be set up to test legally grown and distributed marijuana for potency and contamination.

In short, there will be new administrative, regulatory, and law-enforcement costs of managing legalization, and these will impact budgets at all levels of government.

Medical marijuana regimes are the closest regulatory models we have to a regime of full legalization. But the capacities of states to properly regulate medical marijuana have been greatly tested. In Colorado, a scathing report released in 2013 showed that the state's bureaucracy could not handle its medical marijuana program. An audit found the medical marijuana division "rife with wasteful spending, shoddy enforcement and unfulfilled expectations. Systems that were supposed to track marijuana plants from seed to sale were incomplete. Measures that were supposed to prevent criminals from getting involved in the industry had failed."[11]

5. Tax Evasion Would Be Widespread

"Just because an excise tax is levied does not mean that it will be collected," pointed out the team of analysts who did the 2010 RAND study of how marijuana legalization would affect the California budget. To help determine the extent to which a tax on marijuana might be evaded, they examined relatively recent studies of experiences with tobacco taxes.

A 2000 study in the *British Medical Journal*, for instance, looked at what happened when several Canadian provinces imposed $3 per pack cigarette tax in the 1990s. A black market for untaxed cigarettes and an enormous smuggling problem rapidly developed. The demand for lower-cost untaxed cigarettes soon resulted in 30 percent of all cigarette sales taking place on the black market. As a consequence, these provinces repealed the tax.[12]

California Board of Equalization officials have recently estimated that cigarette excise tax revenue evasion was $182 million in fiscal year 2005–6. Around 15 percent of all cigarettes sold in that state have somehow avoided the excise taxes in place on each pack to raise revenues for the state budget.[13] This is lower than evasion rates in other countries, according to the chief economist for the California Board of Equalization. For example, about 22 percent of the U.K . domestic cigarette market now consists of smuggled cigarettes. In Canada, smuggled cigarettes represented about 33 percent of all domestic cigarette consumption at their peak.[14]

State by state data collected in 2008, indicates that states with the highest excise taxes on each pack or carton of cigarettes also experience the highest rates of tax evasion.[15] This should give us a strong clue about what will happen if and when taxes are imposed on legal marijuana. The case for evasion is stronger for marijuana than for cigarettes, especially because most proposals for taxing marijuana call for considerably greater amounts than the typical $5 an ounce tax on cigarettes. In 2010, the California Board of Equalization estimated that marijuana, taxed at $50 per ounce, could bring in $1.4 billion of revenue for the state. Advocates have touted this as badly needed revenue.

But as the RAND researchers concluded, "Tax revenues could be dramatically lower or higher than the $1.4 billion estimate; for example, there is uncertainty about potential tax revenues that California might derive from taxing marijuana used by residents of other states (e.g., from 'drug tourism')."

The financial incentive to avoid paying marijuana taxes would be so great, especially at proposed levels ($50/ounce in California in 2009 or 25 percent each for processors, retailers, and consumers in Washington in 2012), that the black market in marijuana would equal or even dwarf the underground economy that already exists.

THE REAL BENEFICIARIES OF LEGALIZATION

If not taxpayers or state and local governments, then who would profit most from the legalization of marijuana?

The website Dailyfinance.com did an analysis to identify this list of predictable winners in the marijuana profit game:

- Mainstream tobacco companies: that is firms "that already have a foothold in the smoking market";
- Manufacturers of rolling papers, pipes, and bongs, several of which are also publicly held tobacco companies such as National Tobacco, owner of Zig-Zag rolling papers;
- Junk food providers and major food industry corporations like Kraft Foods (owned, incidentally, by Phillip Morris from 1988 to 2007) are already well positioned to cash in on the "munchies" attacks that typically occur following marijuana consumption.[16]

It could be argued that some additional tax revenue would result from the increased sale of products (e.g., junk food or rolling papers) that are complements to marijuana, though there is no good way to predict how much. We have no reason to believe, however, that such indirect revenues would even come close to matching the total costs of marijuana legalization.

No matter how we look at it, legalizing marijuana will not solve government budgetary woes. If anything, it would make our fiscal situation worse: any revenue gained from taxing this drug would be quickly and substantially offset by the heavy costs associated with its increased prevalence. It's a price we can't afford to bear.

MYTH

6

PORTUGAL AND HOLLAND PROVIDE SUCCESSFUL MODELS OF LEGALIZATION

For decades, American tourists and other visitors knew the Dutch city of Amsterdam as the "San Francisco of Europe," a designation that harkened back to the 1960s "Summer of Love" in San Francisco and reflected Amsterdam's permissive attitudes toward marijuana. The Dutch city emerged as a magnet for foreign "drug tourists" seeking legal highs in "coffee shops" licensed to sell marijuana.

This Dutch experiment has lasted for almost forty years, from 1976, when the possession and sale of up to ninety marijuana cigarettes was decriminalized, to 2011, when awareness of a new reality about marijuana began to dawn on Dutch policymakers and public health authorities. This new awareness emerged because selective breeding has made Dutch marijuana so powerful in its effects that psychiatric problems are cropping up in growing numbers of users. So in October 2011, Holland reclassified strong cannabis (THC of about 15 percent or higher) as a "hard" drug, putting it in the same category as cocaine, and passed a law banning foreign tourists from the nation's seven hundred marijuana coffee shops.[1]

Legalization proponents on this side of the Atlantic have been holding the Dutch experience up for years as a model of rational marijuana policy. Indeed, the Dutch case presents an instructive model for us—but not for the reasons the pro-marijuana movement would have us believe. The about-face in Dutch attitudes and policies provides a cautionary tale for us in the United States as various states consider relaxing their drug laws.

But before examining the Dutch experience in more detail, let's first look at a more recent European experiment that is also at the heart of this myth—the case of Portugal.

IS PORTUGAL A MODEL? IF SO, OF WHAT?

No single country in the last decade has had its drug policy held up on the pro-legalization soapbox more than Portugal. That's because in 2001, the nation passed a law formally decriminalizing all drugs, including marijuana, heroin, and cocaine. When the law was first announced, it sounded extreme on its face and was widely characterized as legalization. Drug legalization advocates cheered.

But just a little bit of digging shows that the Portuguese experience has been vastly exaggerated, twisted, and misused in two principal ways. First, Portugal's policy was decidedly not a form of legalization. Second, the outcomes of the new Portuguese approach are mixed.

DECRIMINALIZATION OR SOMETHING ELSE?

Since 2001, drug users in Portugal have been sent to "dissuasion panels" of social workers, attorneys, and psychiatrists, called Commissions for the Dissuasion of Drug Addiction (Comissões para a Dissuasão da Toxicodependência—CDT). Members of the CDT team assess drug users and refer them to brief health interventions, treatment, a fine, or nothing at all. The policy is in fact similar to the way many European countries have long treated people caught for low-level drug possession. One might even argue that the Portuguese approach is similar to the US drug court or diversion system. One thing is for sure: in no way does the law resemble legalization, or even many reformers' vision of true decriminalization under which users would be slapped with a small (usually uncollected) fine and left alone.

In fact, prior to 2001, Portugal had rarely imprisoned drug users at all. But because of relatively high rates of HIV and other drug-related problems, authorities felt compelled to try a new policy that amped up treatment and intervention strategies, and formally ended any possibility of jail time. In a 2011 profile of the country and its drug-law experiment, the *New Yorker* magazine observed: "Portuguese leaders, flailing about and desperate for change, took an unlikely gamble: they passed a law that made Portugal the first country to fully decriminalize drug use."[2]

Under the new law, drug possession in small amounts became an administrative offense rather than a criminal one. People who are caught using drugs in a public place and/or in possession of a small amount of any drug (up to ten days' worth of personal use) are referred to CDTs. A person *selling* any drug, however, can still be arrested for trafficking, even if the amount in his or her possession is less than ten days' worth.

Portugal's policy is a far cry from legalization, which implies the retail sale, commercial distribution, and production of drugs. But that didn't stop the spin. Misleading headlines and blog posts abounded: "Ten Years of Legalization Has Cut Portugal's Drug Abuse Rate in Half," "What Pot Legalization Looks Like: Portugal Shows the Best Way to Keep Kids Away from Pot Is to Make It Legal for Everyone Else," and "What Happened after Portugal Made All Drugs Legal?" are just a few examples.[3]

To legalization advocates, the details didn't matter. They presented Portugal as a new frontier in legalization and argued that the United States would do well to follow.

WHAT HAS BEEN THE OUTCOME OF PORTUGAL'S POLICY?

The first analysis on Portugal was done in 2009, by the Cato Institute, a libertarian US think tank that has been on record for years favoring the legalization of all drugs.

The Cato report concluded that drug use hadn't increased under decriminalization, that drug-related deaths and HIV rates had fallen, and that generally, things were much better in that country because of the new policy.[4] Immediately after the Cato report was released, its author, a lawyer with no public health research background, went on a world tour promoting his findings. Pro-drug lobby groups and legalization advocates touted Portugal as *the* model of drug policy for the United States. They propped up Portugal as an example of radical revolution in the decades-long drug wars. For example, headlines read, "Portugal Drug Decriminalization: A Resounding Success: Will Britain Respond?"[5]; "Drug Decriminalization Policy Pays Off"[6]; and "5 Years After: Portugal's Drug Decriminalization Policy Shows Positive Results."[7]

In 2011, the *New Yorker* was much more careful in its review of the law's effects: "There is much to debate about the Portuguese approach to drug addiction. Does it help people to quit, or does it transform them into more docile drug addicts, wards of an indulgent state, with little genuine incentive to alter their behavior?"[8]

So what is the straight truth about Portugal and its drug policy? In short, some use and harm levels went up; others went down. And it is questionable whether the policy that Portugal enacted is working as intended.

Depending on which years, age groups, or outcomes one examines, the statistics vary dramatically. The significance of Portugal's experience and the impact of that country's drug policy has been overstated in several ways.

The European Monitoring Centre for Drugs and Drug Addiction (EMCDDA), long considered the authority on drug statistics in Europe, compiled statistics showing an increase in lifetime prevalence rates for the use of cannabis, cocaine, amphetamines, ecstasy, and LSD between 2001 and 2011. Those figures are for the general population of Portugal, ages fifteen to sixty-four years of age.[9] The European School Survey Project on Alcohol and Other Drugs (ESPAD) survey of fifteen- and sixteen-year-olds shows an overall increase in the prevalence of marijuana from 1999 to 2011, although there was an initial dip in use rates. Past-month prevalence for marijuana in that age group went from 5 percent in 1999, to 3 percent in 2003 to 6 percent in 2007, and finally up 9 percent in 2011. EMCDDA concluded that "the most recent ESPAD study corroborates the findings of the [UN World Health Organization] study, showing increasing consumption of illicit substances [in Portugal] since 2006."[10]

Data on the number of drug-related deaths is mixed. Some sources point to an increase in deaths from 280 in 2001, to 314 in 2007.[11] Others point to different numbers, showing data from the General Mortality Registry of the Statistics National Institute in 2010, that twenty-six cases of drug-related deaths occurred in 2010. That represents fewer deaths than the twenty-seven cases reported in 2009 and 2002, but is higher than the number of drug-related deaths reported in each of the years between 2003 and 2008. Clearly, it is a mixed picture.[12] Figure 2 charts data from EMCDDA. As Stanford University Professor Dr. Keith Humphreys notes of the EMCDDA's data, "Portugal decriminalized all drugs in 2001, and these factually accurate data can be used to prove that Portugal's policy has been a complete success or a complete failure, assuming the analyst has no intellectual integrity." Humphreys concludes drolly, "EMCDDA is one of those annoying organizations that provides full information without political spin, so clearly you can't rely on the chart the way they print it up."[13]

With this evidence in hand, the EMCDDA concluded that under

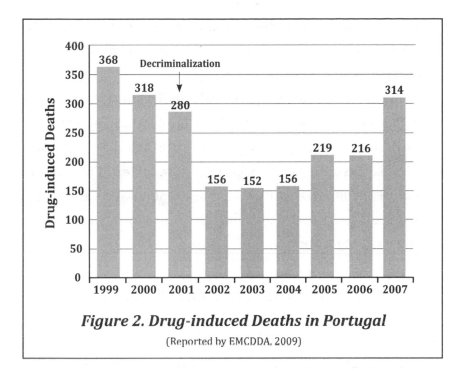

Figure 2. Drug-induced Deaths in Portugal
(Reported by EMCDDA, 2009)

Portugal's drug law "the country still has high levels of problem drug use and HIV infection, and does not show specific developments in its drug situation that would clearly distinguish it from other European countries that have a different policy."[14] The new policy, then, appeared to be neither novel nor a magic bullet.

It's also highly debatable whether Portugal's law has encouraged people with drug problems to seek treatment. As the *New Yorker* article in 2011 pointed out, treatment facilities "became far more accessible just as the new law was passed."[15] Any positive treatment trends and other claimed benefits seen since 2001 may simply be due to increases in treatment capacity and reach. We do not really know.

Indeed, it appears that Portugal's policy isn't really a true decriminalization or legalization strategy. It's more of a treatment- or dissuasion-focused approach similar to those of Portugal's European neighbors.

While the Portuguese experience with drug policy reform extends beyond marijuana, the fact that pro-legalization advocates point to it as a successful model for North American marijuana legalization makes it highly relevant to this context. Close examination has demonstrated that drug legalization advocates in the United States are not strengthening their case by highlighting the Portuguese drug law model.

HOLLAND'S DRAMATIC ABOUT-FACE

A onetime poster child for legalization, Holland has experienced a dramatic about-face in its policies. The Dutch policy began in 1976, not as legalization, but as a nonenforcement policy on marijuana sale and use. (The word *legalization* has never been used by government officials to describe their policy, because such a policy violates Holland's obligations under international law.) The country has made it a practice to looking the other way when marijuana is sold in "coffee shops." When passing the 1976 law, Parliament removed penalties for the possession of thirty grams of marijuana or hashish, an amount that was thought to constitute the average marijuana user's consumption over three months.[16]

In addition to this decriminalization of possession in small amounts, Dutch lawmakers authorized the sale of marijuana and hashish in special "coffee shops" licensed by the government. These shops couldn't sell more than thirty grams to any customer. The import, export, production, or sale of cannabis remained illegal outside of the coffee shops.[17]

From 1976 to the early 1980s, there was little change in Dutch marijuana use levels. Then, when coffee shops started figuring out how much they could profit from the policy by attracting foreigners and advertising their products, the business climate changed. There was a tourism boom, and with the rise in advertising, coffee shops became a favorite destination for foreign tourists and Dutch residents alike. From the mid-1980s to the mid-1990s, the number of coffee shops selling marijuana quintupled.[18]

In 1996, local communities throughout Holland were given the authority to decide whether coffee shops should be allowed within their jurisdictions. Since then, three-quarters of the nearly five hundred local communities in Holland have refused to allow coffee shops to operate within their border at all. As a result, Amsterdam became home to one-third of all coffee shops in the country despite having only 5 percent of the country's population.[19]

But the illegal black market sale of marijuana did not go away in areas with a high concentration of coffee shops legally selling marijuana. There are several reasons for this and all relate to the unfailing opportunism of black market sellers in exploiting the inevitable gaps left open in any regime of legal marijuana. For example, black market dealers take advantage of coffee shops not being open twenty-four hours a day to offer round-the-clock service. Black market sellers also target minors too young to legally enter coffee shops. Additionally, while there are limits on the amount of marijuana a coffee shop visitor can purchase, there is no limit on how much a customer can buy from a black market dealer in a single transaction.[20]

Predictably, as marijuana use was normalized by coffee shops, an increase in marijuana use among Holland's young people occurred. Rates of youth marijuana use more than doubled from the mid-1980s to the mid-1990s. An analysis by a pair of researchers who are sympathetic to marijuana legalization and decriminalization found that the percent of eighteen- to twenty-year-olds reporting marijuana use went from 15 percent in 1984, to 44 percent in 1996, an increase of 300 percent for that age group.[21] The Dutch had always had lower rates of youth marijuana use than the United States, but since the mid-1990s, Dutch rates have caught up to their American counterparts.

Marijuana potency has risen dramatically over the last decade or so. The European Monitoring Centre for Drugs and Drug Addiction has posted statistics showing that THC concentrations in marijuana sold in coffee shops more than doubled between 1999 and 2004, from an average of 8.6 percent in 1999, to more than 20 percent in five years, with an impact on addiction rates and treatment admissions for marijuana.[22]

As potency levels escalated, users began developing a tolerance for the drug, requiring increasingly higher levels of THC to get the same high—a vicious cycle that accelerates the development of dependency. Dutch citizens now are more likely to be admitted to treatment centers for marijuana use than citizens of any other European country.[23]

Holland holds yet another distinction that the pro-marijuana movement might wish would go away. *Foreign Affairs,* published by the US-based Council on Foreign Relations, did an analysis of Holland's drug experiment and described how that country's lenient laws and status as "the drugs capital of western Europe" had turned it into "a magnet for criminal types."[24]

And we're not just talking about marijuana trafficking. Law enforcement authorities in both France and Britain estimated that 80 percent of the heroin used or seized in those countries passed through or was temporarily warehoused in Holland. Most of the amphetamines and ecstasy pills consumed in Europe were manufactured by Dutch traffickers. "Holland has become the place for drug traffickers to work," a British customs official told *Foreign Affairs.* "It's an environment which is relatively trouble-free from a criminal's point of view."[25] To their credit, Dutch law enforcement have begun to fund enforcement operations and intelligence at a much higher rate now than in the past.

Dutch officials did not predict these effects of marijuana legalization. Nor did they predict the sharp increase in use rates, the higher rates of dependency, the significant increase in treatment admission rates, or all of the other social and public health problems that have emerged in Holland over the years.

Observing these effects, however, did eventually drive Dutch lawmakers to reverse their policy. In response to these growing problems, Dutch officials initiated a turnaround, scaling back lenient marijuana laws in late 2011, banning tourists from going to the coffee shops selling marijuana, closing many of the shops, and reclassifying high THC marijuana as a hard drug alongside cocaine. As a *Daily Mail* commentator observed in 2011, Dutch physicians and lawmakers had begun to recognize that marijuana "is very dangerous psychiatrically. Its frequent use leads to an increased incidence of hospitalisation for psychotic breakdown."[26]

Not surprisingly, coffee shop owners have come together as the Cannabis Retailers' Association to take legal action against these changes. They argue, among other things, that these legal changes discriminate against foreigners, who would no longer be able to consume marijuana in their coffee shops. In April 2012, a judge in Holland upheld the new law. Appeals could drag the legal process out for years to come since the cannabis retailers have vowed to take this issue to the European Court of Human Rights .[27]

Certainly, we can learn from Portugal about its public health oriented approach and Holland's warnings about the commercialization of marijuana. But neither Holland nor Portugal represents a successful model of legalization. As I've argued in this chapter, Portugal's policy can hardly be called a legalization regime. And, in any case, the outcomes of Portuguese drug reform are far from resoundingly positive. The Dutch experience, on the other hand, offers a clear warning of the many harms that marijuana legalization can inflict. In the United States, a country obsessed with commercialization in the name of the First Amendment, legalization is sure to be an even riskier proposition.

MYTH

7

PREVENTION, INTERVENTION, AND TREATMENT ARE DOOMED TO FAIL—SO WHY TRY?

A final line of attack mounted by legalization advocates goes something like this: "People have always smoked marijuana and they always will. Why try to stop it?" In other words, since we can't prevent marijuana use (many people continue to smoke marijuana), and since treatment is unnecessary (because marijuana is harmless) and ineffective, why should society engage in a costly and futile exercise aimed at discouraging or restraining use of the drug? Wouldn't it make more sense to legalize marijuana and save society all the costs of prevention, treatment, and enforcement?

This sort of thinking reminds me of the famous line attributed to a US military officer during the Vietnam War: "We had to destroy the village in order to save it." Does the fact that some people will continue to use marijuana (despite its illegality and our best prevention efforts) mean that we should drastically compromise public health by legalizing the drug altogether?

You might also recall this other famous statement about Vietnam, attributed to a US politician: "We should declare victory and leave."[1] Should society just declare "victory" over marijuana use and trafficking by officially condoning or turning a blind eye to these practices, regardless of their long-term costs to public health and safety?

Drug treatment data collected in the United States shows that in 2009, marijuana admissions for treatment exceeded 360,000, a huge jump over the 1992 numbers, when about 93,000 were admitted for treatment to break a marijuana dependency. As I pointed out under the first myth, it's not a coincidence that the jump in treatment numbers corresponds to the drastic rise in the THC potency of marijuana. THC potency in the United States went from an average of 3 percent in 1992, to 14 percent by 2011—a 500 percent increase that has transformed modern marijuana into an irrefutably harmful substance.[2,3] Treatment and emergency room admissions related to marijuana use have also significantly increased over the last fifteen years.[4]

Such high numbers of admissions for marijuana treatment due to stronger marijuana mean that unless intervention and prevention strategies are correspondingly scaled up, public health agencies will be battling this problem for many decades to come. In this sense, legalization proponents are right—the prevention, intervention, and treatment of cannabis-related problems are and will remain a challenging social endeavor. But it is not, by any means, a "pointless" one.

PREVENTING MARIJUANA USE

A large body of research shows how and why drug use is initiated, and which factors in a person's life act as protection against use. Much of this research focuses on youths at various stages, from childhood to adolescence.[5]

The National Institute on Drug Abuse (NIDA), an arm of the National Institutes of Health, has compiled the most important research on marijuana prevention and produced a chart reflecting the primary risk and protective factors in five key domains of a person's life—individual, family, peer group, school, and community.[6]

Table 2. Primary Risk and Protective Factors in Marijuana Use Prevention

Risk Factors	Domain	Protective Factors
Early Aggressive Behavior	Individual	Self-Control
Lack of Parental Supervision	Family	Parental Monitoring
Substance Abuse	Peer	Academic Competance
Drug Availability	School	Anti–drug Use Policies

We can safely say that as a child is exposed to more of these risk factors, his or her probability of future drug abuse goes up. Likewise, exposure to protective factors decreases the likelihood of eventual drug abuse.

There is also a strong association between a parent's drug and alcohol use and subsequent use by the child. Peer group drug usage plays an important role, as do cultural attitudes that drug use should be tolerated. Children and teenagers who display impulsive behaviors are at a higher risk of initiating drug use, as are children in stressful environments marked by violence and crime.[7,8]

Strong parent-child bonding, good family communication skills, and a family structure based on clear and consistent discipline act as protective factors. An additional protective influence is provided by religious or spiritual values in the family. Further protection can be provided by the school and classroom environment where goals and values are instilled or reinforced, and teachers intervene to diminish negative peer group interactions.[9]

Youths at high risk for drug abuse *are not* just a product of low-income dysfunctional family settings and high-crime environments. Studies done in the United States and France found that youths in affluent families often experiment with marijuana, perhaps because of their disposable income. These youths, however, are not as likely to become addicted, possibly because they tend to be more careful and concerned about not undermining their school performance and long-term career prospects.[10,11]

Based on all of this research, we can say that youths who have multiple risk factors for marijuana abuse and few protective factors are most vulnerable for developing lifelong problems with marijuana abuse and addiction. Youths in this category are also more likely to drop out of school and become jobless.

We also know from numerous studies that perception of risk is extremely important in discouraging abuse. As youths (and adults) become more educated and aware that marijuana use carries health risks, their use declines and overall social disapproval intensifies. This is documented in US school survey data produced by the *Monitoring the Future National Survey Results on Drug Use, 1975-1998*: "The amount of perceived risk associated with cannabis fell during the earlier period of increased use in the late-1970s, and fell again during the more recent resurgence of use in the 1990s. Again, perceived risk was a leading indicator of change in use, as it has been proven to be for a number of drugs."[12]

Education about the health dangers of marijuana use is the key to increasing perceived risk, just as prevention is key to lowering the long-term costs to society of drug treatment. It has been estimated that for every dollar we invest in drug use prevention efforts, up to $10 is saved in treatment costs.[13]

What are the most successful approaches to prevention? NIDA, which is estimated to fund 85 percent of all research on drug abuse throughout the world, has identified these core principles:

- Successful prevention programs promote parental monitoring of children, bonding between parents and children, participation and success in school and extracurricular activities.
- These programs focus on reducing risk factors for drug abuse, including academic failure, caregivers as substance abusers, peer group deviancy, availability of drugs in the community, and poli-

cies and attitudes that promote the normalization of drug use.

- Effective programs are localized and community specific, and tailored for target audiences. This means that risk factors unique to each community become a focal point of education.
- Prevention programs need to be implemented with a consistent message in multiple settings simultaneously, which might include schools, churches, service organizations, and youth groups, such as Boy Scouts and Girl Scouts.
- Drug-free community coalitions (more on these in the next section) can help to facilitate comprehensive approaches. Communities with such coalitions have shown significant reductions in cannabis use among middle school- and high school-age youth.
- Another important feature of successful programs is an emphasis on teaching parents and children life skills and behavior skills (often using behavior skills games) that enhance self-control and self-esteem.[14]

It's important that education efforts effectively emphasize the many health-related dangers of cannabis use: that one in eleven cannabis users (one in six among kids) will become dependent, that addiction produces serious withdrawal symptoms, and that marijuana use can affect learning and economic outcomes.[15]

Drug-policy researchers have been pessimistic about the value of prevention. Indeed, systematic reviews show that only a small handful of school-based programs are successful in providing long-term protection against the initiation of drug use. But what is missing in many of these evaluations is attention to comprehensive, community-based approaches—approaches that not only implement classroom lessons, but engage the entire community to make environmental and policy changes based on local data and specific needs.

An early illustration of this comprehensive approach comes from the crack-cocaine epidemic of the 1980s, when groups from a variety of sectors—government leaders, teachers, social workers, parents, law enforcement, business owners, and faith-based communities—banded together to shut down open-air drug markets, apprehend violent drug dealers, and educate youths about the harms of crack use. These partnerships—or coalitions—emphasized altering the physical environment where drug use occurs (e.g., improving lighting in public areas), changing local laws and ordinances related to drug use (e.g., limiting liquor outlet density in a neighborhood), and introducing incentives and disincentives to alter consequences of a specific behavior (e.g., increasing public recognition in the community for healthy behavior).[16] As part of a strategic plan to achieve population-level reductions in substance abuse, such an approach employs interventions that are focused both on the individual and the environment.

COMMUNITY DRUG PREVENTION PROGRAMS DEMONSTRATE VALUE

In 1989, just a few months after the inauguration of George H.W. Bush, America's new president called up his friend Tom Landry, who had just stepped down as the beloved coach of the Dallas Cowboys. Coach Landry was probably best known for having invented the most commonly used defense in modern American football. Football strategies, however, were not the subject of this conversation.

The president was more interested in an offensive against drugs.

Drugs, of course, preoccupied the consciousness of most Americans at that time—as crack cocaine wreaked havoc in neighborhoods across the country, surveys consistently ranked drugs as the number one policy concern of voters.[17] While President Bush was a strong supporter of DARE and other 1980s-style prevention programs, he wanted to make a break from the Reagans' "Just Say No" campaign. He had heard about "community action groups" springing up to fight crack cocaine.

These groups harnessed the power of the community's business, labor, faith-based, and social services sectors to customize prevention programs based on local data and specific community needs. President Bush asked Coach Landry, and others like Alvah Chapman, the former chair of Knight-Ridder, and Jim Burke, the former chair of Johnson & Johnson, to come up with some fresh ideas about how to improve this growing movement of community-based prevention. They and twenty-four others became known as the President's Drug Advisory Council, and Bush gave them a two-year deadline to come up with major recommendations.

The Council noted that small community-based groups—by now they called themselves drug-free community coalitions—were already being formed in localities all across the nation. Rather than implementing one-shot, individual drug-prevention programs, these newly formed coalitions were bringing different sectors of society around a table to discuss local problems and to form community action groups. Resulting initiatives included neighborhood anticrime task forces to close down a violent open-air drug market; business-led drug-free workplace initiatives, and local legislative campaigns to tighten liquor store zoning laws.

While the president's council liked what it saw, it observed one major weakness in this existing local approach: the lack of an umbrella organization supporting community coalitions education materials, cutting-edge training, and public policy backing at the national level.

Two years later, when the president summoned his Council for a report, the major recommendation, unsurprisingly, was to create a national umbrella organization for the some nine hundred coalitions that had sprouted up across the country. In October 1992, Community Anti-Drug Coalitions of America (CADCA) was born. President Bush promised that, regardless of the outcome of the 1992 presidential election, "this group is going to work with business, with labor, with community leaders."

Indeed, since 1992, CADCA, based in Arlington, Virginia, has been at the forefront of developing local, targeted approaches to substance abuse and related problems. As of this writing, more than five thousand of these community coalitions exist in the United States, thanks in large measure to CADCA's organizational, educational, and technical assistance.

To illustrate the impact that community coalition education campaigns can have on local marijuana use rates, data is often compiled based on comparative local school and national marijuana use surveys. Here are a few examples:

■ In Sylvania, Ohio, marijuana use decreased by nearly 50 percent among tenth graders in the decade following 2002 (three times more than the drop in the national average over that period), as a result of a community youth leadership training program, education to raise awareness about the health risks of marijuana, and collaboration with local schools to implement policies that keep marijuana out of educational settings.[18]

- In Ashland, Kentucky, marijuana use among twelfth graders has fallen 27.3 percent since 2004, according to a survey by Monitoring the Future. These usage decreases in Ashland were attributed to wide dissemination of educational materials throughout the community and a program specifically targeting a change in "social norms" surrounding drug use.[19]

- In Jackson County, Kansas, tenth graders decreased their marijuana use by 47.7 percent between 2005 and 2010, due to an effective community coalition campaign that involved education, a science-based prevention program in two grade levels of each school district in the county, and a proactive effort to identify and monitor vacant buildings and other sites where students were congregating to smoke marijuana and initiate their peers into the practice.[20]

These local examples are consistent with a recent evaluation of middle school youth living in the United States. In 2010, an independent evaluation found that communities with such coalitions had significant reductions in alcohol, tobacco, and cannabis use among middle school- and high school-age youth, while perception of the risks associated with these drugs increased among youth.[21] This confirms previously published research showing positive results from coalitions that enact environmental policies aimed at reducing drug availability and access among youth.[22]

MYTH 7

THE "GATEWAY" DEBATE: WHY IT MATTERS AND WHY IT DOESN'T

When the Boomer generation was in high school during the 1960s and 1970s, their education from authority figures concerning the dangers of marijuana focused almost entirely on a "gateway" theory about the drug: if you smoke marijuana, you will inevitably try cocaine or heroin, become an addict, and ruin your life. Once many Boomers discovered from firsthand experience that trying marijuana didn't automatically result in cocaine or heroin addiction, their cynicism about drug education in general, and marijuana education, in particular, became epidemic.

Although most people who use marijuana will not go on to use other drugs, it is indisputable that users of illegal drugs other than marijuana almost always begin with marijuana. A famous French study of almost thirty thousand teenagers, for example, shows a correlation between marijuana use and the use of other drugs. The French study concluded that experimenting with marijuana increases the risk of using other drugs by a factor of twenty-one. Tobacco and alcohol initiation, in turn, were shown to be associated with a greater likelihood of using marijuana.[23] Another study by Yale University researchers in 2012 published in the *Journal of Adolescent Health*, showed that alcohol, cigarettes, and marijuana were associated with an increased likelihood of prescription drug abuse in men eighteen to twenty-five. In women of that age, only marijuana use was linked with a higher likelihood of prescription drug abuse. The study didn't show an association between alcohol or cigarette use in young women and later use of prescription drugs.[24]

Furthermore, in 2003, Australian researchers published a major study of 311 same-sex twins in the *Journal of the American Medical Association.* Each pair had one twin that had used marijuana before age seventeen and one twin who had never used the drug. The researchers found that the marijuana-using siblings were five times more likely than their nonusing twins to go on to hallucinogens like LSD; three times more likely to go on to cocaine; and twice as likely to go on to heroin.[25] Citing similar findings, Robert MacCoun and Peter Reuter conclude, "the evidence for a correlation between marijuana use and hard drug use is...overwhelming."[26]

But the more interesting question is: *why* does marijuana precede other drug use? Is the relationship a causal one? That answer is unclear. Some have posited that an initial pleasurable experience with marijuana encourages the use of other drugs by users seeking better and different highs. Others have argued that obtaining marijuana from the black market requires coming into contact with dealers who might then push drugs other than marijuana. These different accounts come with different policy implications. If the first mechanism is correct, then it is important to restrict marijuana use in order to prevent users from coming to desire other highs. If the second is correct, policies should aim to "separate" drug markets (e.g., making marijuana legal while keeping cocaine illegal) so that marijuana users do not come into contact with users and dealers of other drugs.

Neither mechanism provides a justification for legalization, however. The illegality of marijuana reduces the likelihood of its use relative to legal drugs. And most marijuana users today obtain their drugs from familiar sources such as friends and acquaintances, not through contact with aggressive dealers who might have other drugs to sell.[27, 28]

RAND researchers have offered an altogether different, non-causal explanation for the fact that people use marijuana before going on to harder drugs. Their analysis of drug use patterns reported by more than fifty-eight thousand US residents between the ages of twelve and twenty-five shows that those who use drugs may have an underlying drug use propensity that is *not specific to any one drug*. They write: "The presence of a common propensity could explain why people who use one drug are so much more likely to use another than are people who do not use the first drug. It has also been suggested that marijuana use precedes hard-drug use simply because opportunities to use marijuana come earlier in life than opportunities to use hard drugs." The authors conclude that, "The research does not disprove the gateway theory; it merely shows that another explanation is plausible."[29]

Why people use marijuana before initiating the use of other substances such as cocaine remains unclear. On the one hand, understanding the mechanism driving this pattern is important: understanding the role of marijuana in the context of broader drug use will help us craft more effective drug policies. But the harms of marijuana use—and therefore, our interest in preventing and treating the use of that drug—should not be tied to its status as a so-called gateway drug. The consequences of marijuana use are in and of themselves significant enough to warrant concern, regardless of gateway status or any particular gateway mechanism that might be at play.

PROVEN MARIJUANA TREATMENT STRATEGIES

When prevention fails to stop marijuana use from happening in the first place, interventions and treatment may be necessary. Though medical research continues, we currently don't have any medications to assist in the treatment of cannabis dependency the way we do for heroin.

Numerous treatment approaches, however, have demonstrated effectiveness. These range from interventions using cognitive behavioral therapy to other techniques including motivational incentives that reward users who successfully remain abstinent.[30] Let's take a closer look at these treatments.

Cognitive Behavioral Therapy (CBT) is a type of psychotherapy, designed to treat life problems and develop self-control by changing thought patterns. It focuses on finding solutions to problem emotions, behaviors, and thoughts by enabling the person to understand how his or her thinking became distorted.[31] Through an interactive question-and-answer session with a therapist, clients discover how to trace the cause-and-effect patterns produced by their minds and how certain thoughts trigger compulsive behaviors. The goal is to learn to alter those thoughts at will.

By self-monitoring, a person using CBT can anticipate likely triggers for the desire to use marijuana and then utilize a coping strategy to short-circuit the cravings. Research studies indicate that once CBT treatment is complete, the skills learned continue to be used indefinitely.[32]

In a study of 450 marijuana-dependent people undergoing CBT to break their marijuana habits, it was found that "a nine-session individual approach that integrated CBT and motivational interviewing" was effective in the initiation and maintenance of marijuana cessation. Similar studies of alcohol and other drug abusers have demonstrated that CBT is not only effective, but "durable and that continuing improvement may occur even after the end of treatment."[33]

Motivational Interviewing (sometimes referred to as *Motivational Enhancement Therapy)* can best be described as a brief intervention with a chronic user, usually conducted by a licensed therapist or counselor, designed to produce a rapid, internally motivated change in behavior. These are nonconfrontational encounters (unlike the kind of confrontational interventions usually portrayed in reality television shows) to help facilitate in the client a willingness to change and seek treatment for a marijuana use problem. The therapist uses motivational interviewing principles to help the user weigh the pros and cons of marijuana use, to strengthen the user's motivation for change, and then to build a plan for that change. By adding family members to this process, the chances for success are improved, particularly among adolescent users.[34,35] This approach is more effective when combined with CBT sessions to create a comprehensive intervention and treatment approach.

Contingency Management Interventions involve offering incentives (praise or small gifts) to users for changing their behavior and maintaining abstinence from drug use (verified by urine tests). These incentives can range from small amounts of money to vouchers for movie passes, food, or other goods and services. NIDA notes that studies show "incentive-based interventions are highly effective in increasing treatment retention and promoting abstinence from drugs.[36]

A study in 2006, randomly placed ninety cannabis-dependent adults in either a CBT group, an abstinence-based voucher incentive group, or a group that was a combination of the two approaches. Treatment lasted fourteen weeks. Results indicated that a program of abstinence-based vouchers was "a potent treatment option," and that CBT "enhanced the post-treatment maintenance of the initial positive effect of vouchers on abstinence."[37]

TWELVE-STEP RECOVERY PROGRAMS

Unbeknownst to many, Marijuana Anonymous (MA) groups exist around the world, similar to AA groups that have now become part of the fabric of America. Like AA, MA relies on a twelve-step recovery model that emphasizes peer support and honesty. An article by Dr. George Valliant summed it up best about AA, which can be applied to MA: "The reason that AA succeeds...is that AA involves the subcortical brain (A.K.A. the 'heart') and modern medicine does not. There are two principles that Alcoholics Anonymous (AA) and its Twelve Steps use to affect the subcortical brain: first, its emphasis on admitting powerlessness, leading to the positive emotion of love and second, the recognition that to keep it you have to give it away leading to the positive emotion of joy. Both principles are counter-intuitive and militate against the world of cognitive enlightenment that has taken over modern rational medicine since the 18th Century. The only outcome that makes a lasting difference in the devastating disease...is lifelong abstinence. This is what AA strives for and often eventually succeeds in effecting."

What is the remission rate for people who have undergone treatment for marijuana dependency? Researchers in 2010 reviewed dozens of studies on drug remission from throughout the world. They defined remission as being abstinent or no longer dependent for three years after treatment. In the case of marijuana, between 36 percent and 82 percent of users turned out to be no longer dependent on marijuana, depending on the study and the statistics used.[38] This compares favorably to remission rates for many other drugs, including cocaine, for which the upper bound of the remission rate was 58 percent in a comprehensive review of all studies.

Taken together, the evidence indicates that marijuana addiction is both preventable and treatable. This does not mean, of course, that *all* marijuana use can be prevented. To imply that the worthiness of prevention and treatment requires a 100 percent success rate is, of course, ridiculous. That marijuana use persists does not detract from the fact that significant numbers of people can and do avoid using the drug because of evidence-based prevention and treatment.

Despite the evidence, we have never engaged in a truly comprehensive prevention and treatment effort in the United States. We owe it to ourselves to try such an approach before gambling on a policy as risky as legalization.

A SMART APPROACH FOR MARIJUANA POLICY

In the United States, marijuana policy brings with it a lot of baggage. For many Americans, marijuana laws conjure up thoughts of police coercion, social injustice, and hysterical propaganda. Some have had innocuous personal experiences using the drug; others have had (or have heard about) disproportionately negative experiences with the social justice system as a result of marijuana use. For all of these reasons, having a rational discussion about marijuana policy is very challenging in this country.

A smart approach on marijuana policy means putting old ideas and biases aside. It starts with recognizing the health problems caused by the drug, while shifting the emphasis of policy away from either legalization *or* excessive punitiveness to one of prevention, education, health care, treatment, and effective criminal justice programs.

Many people recognize that state governments have been too

hard on marijuana users in the past, and this colors perceptions of what our policies should be in the present. We cannot undo the excesses of the past. But we must make sure that an arrest for marijuana today doesn't end up ruining—or even limiting—somebody's life down the road.

If carried out correctly, however, arrests can serve two good purposes. A smart arrest policy can both provide a societal stamp of disapproval and provide an opportunity to intervene and stop the progression of use. The current policy of simply arresting and fining marijuana users represents a missed opportunity for drug education and intervention.

In some jurisdictions, an arrest record will follow the arrestee forever, preventing that person from rebuilding a better life. Depriving people with an arrest record from a full and meaningful engagement with society can be counterproductive: it can make them feel disconnected from their social and economic environment, increasing their desire to use and/or their need to sell drugs in order to survive. Some states have started to recognize the need for fairness and balance in arrest policy. In New Jersey, for instance, a 2008 law expunges criminal records for first marijuana offenses, if arrestees enter and complete supervisory treatment.

There is no doubt that current policy leaves much to be desired. Today's marijuana policies leave us with a substantial abuse problem, $15–$30 billion in illegal revenues, a product of unknown quality that is accessible to youths, and arrest records for many people (and disproportionally, people of color) whose most serious crime is smoking marijuana. But we don't have to live in an all-or-nothing world. There are smart, sensible solutions that steer clear of policy extremes.

AFTERWORD

Marijuana may not be as harmful as cocaine or heroin—and marijuana legalization is not equivalent to the legalization of harder drugs—but marijuana is also not the harmless herb touted by many legalization advocates. A better marijuana policy would focus on public health strategies and outcomes, namely prevention, intervention, treatment, and a wise use of enforcement resources. Investments in prevention and early intervention that get healthcare professionals and others involved in kids' lives enable us to identify early use before it becomes more harmful chronic use. Some sort of legal sanction should remain in place simply to act as a deterrent and send a social message with the intent of discouraging use—for example, smart criminal penalties grounded in swift, but modest, sanctions. But we can't afford to rely exclusively on the criminal justice system to address a problem of public health.

PROJECT SAM—SMART APPROACHES TO MARIJUANA

When it comes to marijuana policy, our only choices are not strict prohibition or lax legalization. A smart balance can be struck between the extremes of either "tough" or "lenient" marijuana law policies. That is why former Rhode Island congressman Patrick J. Kennedy and I started a new group called Project SAM—Smart Approaches to Marijuana (www.learnaboutsam.org). Project SAM is a collaboration of individuals and organizations seeking marijuana policy that neither incarcerates people with small amounts of marijuana nor creates a profit-driven commercial marijuana industry that aggressively markets the drug. Our desired marijuana policy would reduce marijuana use through prevention, treatment, and smart justice, but it would not cripple marijuana users and low-level dealers with career-ending arrest or incarceration records.

This commonsense approach relies on science, public health, and public safety principles to guide marijuana policy. And several public health physicians and professionals have already joined SAM's board, including Denver-based treatment expert and researcher Dr. Paula Riggs, Harvard University's Dr. Sharon Levy, marijuana treatment specialist Dr. Christian Thurstone, tobacco cessation expert and University of Kansas professor Dr. Kimber Richter, Boston Children's Hospital researcher Dr. Sion Kim Harris, Seattle Children's Hospital physician and adolescent physician Dr. Leslie Walker, President of the Colorado Chapter of the American Academy of Pediatrics Dr. Kathryn Wells, and recovery advocate Ben Cort.

Legalization opens the door to the development of a massive commercial industry that would target and addict the young and the poor, continuously invent new products to capture segmented markets, steadfastly deny that its products cause any harm to health, safety, or well-being, and make so much money that multibillion-dollar lawsuits would simply be the normal cost of doing business.

And we certainly don't need to legalize marijuana to make it available to patients with serious or terminal illnesses. We can speed up research into marijuana's components as potential medicines. Until new products reach the market, we can provide nonintoxicating extracts of marijuana, like CBD, to those under meaningful physician oversight who have a serious and legitimate need. This can be done today, through existing legal pathways.

Some more specific policy proposals follow.

AFTERWORD

Goals of Marijuana Policy

- To have an honest conversation about marijuana and the science behind today's high-potency product.
- To reduce the harms of both marijuana use and the laws designed to prevent its use.
- To treat low-level, nonviolent marijuana arrestees in a way that does not jeopardize their future chances of getting a job or college loan.
- To promote research on marijuana in order to obtain FDA-approved, pharmacy-dispensed marijuana-based medications. In the meantime, kick-start a compassionate use FDA program of nonsmoked, nonpsychoactive cannabis components/extracts made available to seriously ill patients who lack other treatment options.
- To prevent a "Joe Camel" scenario where Big Marijuana competes for the youth market.
- To ensure that the gargantuan alcohol and tobacco industries do not diversify to grow, distribute, market, or sell marijuana.

Marijuana Use/Possession Laws

SAM believes in the fair treatment of individuals who use marijuana and/or possess small amounts of the drug. Specifically, SAM recommends:

- That possession or use of a small amount of marijuana be an offense subject to a health evaluation, resulting (depending on need) in a marijuana education program, a mandatory health screening, referral to treatment, and/or referral to social support services (e.g., job training).

■ That offenders be monitored in the community for six to twelve months for further drug use.

■ Smoke-free laws applying to tobacco are extended to marijuana.

■ Criminal records for small amounts of marijuana are expunged.

Production, Distribution, Dealing, and Sale of Larger Amounts of Marijuana

SAM seeks fair and proportionate penalties for these crimes and recommends:

■ That they remain misdemeanors or felonies based on amounts possessed.

■ An end to mandatory minimum sentences so that judges can exercise discretion under the law.

■ Assessment and mandatory treatment in prison for those who are addicted, with appropriate aftercare upon release.

■ Restoration of all civil rights once misdemeanor marijuana offenders have served sentences.

■ Services for reentry into the community through Justice Reinvestment and similar programs.

Marijuana and Driving

SAM seeks to keep America's roadways safe for all drivers. Because no bodily fluid level of THC (or metabolites) denoting impairment has yet been established, it recommends that:

- Driving with marijuana in one's system is a misdemeanor offense. Repeat offenses need harsher punishments. If any driving results in injury, harsher and swifter penalties must apply.
- Driving under the influence of any amount of marijuana result in a mandatory health assessment, marijuana-education program, and/or referral to treatment or social services.

America is being sold a false dichotomy: "We can either stick to our current failed policies, or we can try a 'new approach' with legalization." Sadly, this kind of black-and-white thinking conceals the fact that there are better, more effective ways than either legalization or incarceration to deal with this complex issue.

A shift to the smart marijuana policy I am proposing will have many benefits. Children and adolescents will be protected from the inevitable commercialization of marijuana that would result from legalization, keeping use and the harms of early initiation to a minimum. The negative consequences of arresting people who possess small amounts of marijuana would be greatly diminished. And non-smoked, cannabis-based medicines would be *prescribed* by physicians and sold in pharmacies rather than at medical marijuana "dispensaries." Marijuana legalization, though seductive, has no place in a policy based on health, safety, and common sense. Neither does hysteria. It is time for reefer sanity.

FOOTNOTES

INTRODUCTION

1. Musto, D. (1999). *The American Disease: Origins of Narcotic Control.* (Expanded ed.) New York: Oxford University Press.

2. Colao, J. (2013, March 26). Meet the Yale MBAs trying to tame the marijuana industry. *Forbes.* Retrieved from http://www.forbes.com/sites/jjcolao/2013/03/26/meet-the-yale-mbas-trying-to-tame-the-marijuana-industry.

3. Ingold, J. (2013, March 31). Marijuana tourism company launches in Colorado after pot legalization. *Daily Freeman.* Retrieved from http://www.dailyfreeman.com/articles/2013/03/31/blotter/story_15a334c2-a859-4186-a884-a1a2da4c0551.txt.

MYTH 1

1. St. Pierre, A. (2012, February 27). Personal communication, message to Dr. K. Sabet. E-mail.

2. U.S. Congress. House of Representatives. Committee on Ways and Means. 1937. *Taxation on Marihuana.* 75th Congress, 1st sess., 27-30 April, 4 May.

3. Owen, J. (2007, March 18). Cannabis: An apology. *Independent*. Retrieved from http://www.independent.co.uk/life-style/health-and-families/health-news/cannabis-an-apology-440730.html.

4. Smith, E.D. (2010, April 20). My changing perspectives: A 45-year view from the Haight-Ashbury. *Marijuana & money: A CNBC special report*. Retrieved from http://www.cnbc.com/id/36180874.

5. Smith, D.E. (1998). Foreword in *The truth about pot*, by J. Baum. Minnesota: Hazelden.

6. Meserve, J. and Ahlers, M.M. (2009, May 14). Marijuana potency surpasses 10 percent, U.S. says. *CNN*. Retrieved from http://www.cnn.com/2009/HEALTH/05/14/marijuana.potency/index.html?iref=allsearch.

7. Substance Abuse and Mental Health Services Administration, Center for Behavioral Health Statistics and Quality. (2011). Drug abuse warning network, 2008: National estimates of drug-related emergency department visits. *HHS Publication* No. SMA 11-4618. Rockville, MD.

8. Compton, W.M. et al. (2004). Prevalence of marijuana use disorders in the United States: 1991-1992 and 2001-2002. *Journal of the American Medical Association, 291*(17), 2114-2121.

9. Maldonado, R. et al. (2011). Neurochemical basis of marijuana addiction. *Neuroscience, 181*, 1-17.

10. Fisar, Z. (2009). Phytocannabidoids and endocannabidoids. *Current Drug Abuse Review, 2*, 51-75.

11. National Institute on Drug Abuse, National Institutes of Health. (2010, September). How does marijuana use affect your brain and body? Retrived from http://www.drugabuse.gov/publications/marijuana-abuse/how-does-marijuana-use-affect-your-brain-body.

12. Herkenham, M. et al. (1990). Cannabinoid receptor localization in the brain. *Proceedings of the National Academy of Sciences, USA, 87*(5), 1932-1936.

13. Pope, H.G. et al. (2001). Neuropsychological performance in

long-term cannabis users. *Archives of General Psychiatry, 58*(10), 909-915.

14. Anthony, J.C., Warner, L.A., Kessler, R.C. (1994). Comparative epidemiology of dependence on tobacco, alcohol, controlled substances, and inhalants: Basic findings from the National Cormorbidity Survey. *Experiential and Clinical Psychopharmacology, 2,* 244.

15. Budney, A.J. et al. (2008). Comparison of cannabis and tobacco withdrawl: Severity and contribution to relapse. *Journal of Substance Abuse Treatment, 35*(4), 362-368.

16. Kolb, B. et al. (2006). Chronic treatment with Delta-9-tetrahydrocannabinol alters the structure of neurons in the nucleus accumbens shell and medial prefrontal cortex of rats. *Synapse, 60*(6), 429-436.

17. Tanda, G. et al. (2003). Cannabinoids: Reward, dependence, and underlying neurochemical mechanisms – A review of recent preclinical data. *Psychopharmacology, 169*(2), 115-134.

18. Anthony. (1994). Comparative epidemiology of dependence.

19. Herkenham, M. et al. (1990). Cannabinoid receptor localization.

20. Tan, W.C. et al. (2009). Marijuana and chronic obstructive lung disease: A population-based study. *Canadian Medical Association Journal, 180*(8), 814-820.

21. Substance Abuse and Mental Health Services Administration, Office of Applied Studies. (2009). Treatment episode data set (TEDS): 2009 discharges from substance abuse treatment services, DASIS. Retrieved from http://www.samhsa.gov/data/2k12/TEDS2009N/TEDS09DWeb.pdf.

22. California Society of Addiction Medicine. (2009, September). Impact of marijuana on children and adolescents: CSAM WEBSITE evidence-based information on cannabis/marijuana. Retrieved from http://www.csam-asam.org/sites/default/files/impact_of_marijuana_on_children_and_adolescents.pdf.

23. Fergusson, D.M. et al. (2003). Cannabis and educational achievements. *Addiction, 98(*12), 1681-1692.

24. Patton, G.C. et al. (2002). Cannabis use and mental health in young people: cohort study. *British Medical Journal, 325*(7374), 1195-1198.

25. Limonero, J.T. et al. (2006). Perceived emotional intelligence and its relation to tobacco and cannabis use among university students. *Psicothema, 18*(Suppl.), 95-100.

26. Yucel, M. et al. (2008). Regional brain abnormalities associated with long-term heavy cannabis use. *Archives of General Psychiatry, 65*(6), 694-701.

27. Schweinsburg, A.D. et al. (2008). The influence of marijuana use on neurocognitive functioning in adolescents. *Current Drug Abuse Review, 1*(1), 99-111.

28. Solowij, N. et al. (2008). The chronic effects of cannabis on memory in humans: A review. *Current Drug Abuse Review, 1*(1), 98.

29. Solowij, N. et al. (2002). Cognitive functioning of long-term heavy cannabis users seeking treatment. *Journal of the American Medical Association, 287*(9), 1123-1131.

30. Salleh. A. (2013, January 23). Cannabis, IQ link more than socioeconomics. *ABC Science*. Retrieved from http://www.abc.net.au/science/articles/2013/01/23/3674424.htm#.UaY20kBkzzg.

31. Science Media Center. (2013). Teen cannabis IQ impact questioned – experts respond. Retrieved from http://www.sciencemediacentre.co.nz/2013/01/15/teen-cannabis-iq-impact-questioned-experts-respond/.

32. Andreasson, S. et al. (1987). Cannabis and schizophrenia: A longitudinal study of Swedish conscripts. *Lancet, 2*(8574), 1483-1486.

33. Moore, T.H. et al. (2007). Cannabis use and risk of psychotic or affective mental health outcomes: A systematic review. *Lancet, 370*(9584), 319-328.

FOOTNOTES

34. Large, M. et al. (2011). Cannabis use and earlier onset of psychosis: A systematic meta-analysis. *Archives of General Psychiatry, 68*(6), 555-561.

35. Harley, M. et al. (2010). Cannabis use and childhood trauma interact additively to increase the risk of psychotic symptoms in adolescence. *Psychological Medicine, 40*(10), 1627-1634.

36. Lynch, M.J. et al. (2012, January 12). The cannabis-psychosis link. *Psychiatric Times.* Retrieved from http://www.psychiatrictimes.com/schizophrenia/content/article/10168/2017327.

37. California Society of Addiction Medicine. (2009, September). Impact of marijuana on children.

38. American Lung Association. (2012, November 27). Health hazards of smoking marijuana. Retrieved from http://www.lung.org/stop-smoking/about-smoking/health-effects/marijuana-smoke.html.

39. Tashkin, D.P. et al. (2002). Respiratory and immunologic consequences of marijuana smoking. *Journal of Clinical Pharmacology, 42*(11 Suppl.), 71S-81S.

40. Moore, B.A. et al. (2005). Respiratory effects of marijuana and tobacco use in a U.S. sample. *Journal General Internal Medicine, 20*(1), 33-37.

41. Tetrault, J.M. et al. (2007). Effects of marijuana smoking on pulmonary function and respiratory complications: A systematic review. *Archives of Internal Medicine, 167(*3), 221-228.

42. Aldington, S. et al. (2007). Effects of cannabis on pulmonary structure, function and symptoms. *Thorax, 62*(12), 1058-1063.

43. Tan, W.C. et al. (2009). Marijuana and chronic obstructive lung disease.

44. National Institute on Drug Abuse, National Institutes of Health. (2010, November). Marijuana. Retrived from http://www.drugabuse.gov/drugs-abuse/marijuana.

45. Jouanjus, E. et al. (2011). Cannabis-related hospitalizations:

Unexpected serious events identified through hospital databases. *British Journal of Clinical Pharmacology, 71*(5), 758-765.

46. Dwivedi, S. et al. (2008). Cannabis smoking and acute coronary syndrome: Two illustrative cases. *International Journal of Cardiology, 128*(2), 54-57.

47. Sattout, A.H. et al. (2009). Cardiac arrest following cannabis use: A case report. *Cases Journal, 2,* 208.

48. Mittleman, M.A. et al. (2001). Triggering myocardial infarction by marijuana. *Circulation, 103*(23), 2805-2809.

49. Wolff, V. et al. (2011). Cannabis use, ischemic stroke, and multifocal intracranial vasoconstriction: A prospective study in 48 consecutive young patients. *Stroke, 42(6)*, 1778-1780.

50. Sidney, S. (2002). Cardiovascular consequences of marijuana use. *Journal of Clinical Pharmacology, 42*(11 Suppl.), 64S-70S.

51. Schmid, K. et al. (2010). The effects of cannabis on heart rate variability and well-being in young men. *Pharmacopsychiatry, 43*(4), 147-150.

52. Roberts, C. (2013, March 13). Thanks to 'dabbing,' it is possible to overdose on marijuana. *SFWeekly*. Retrieved from http://blogs.sfweekly.com/thesnitch/2013/03/medical_marijuana_overdose_dabbing.php.

53. Roberts, C. (2013, March 13). Thanks to 'dabbing.'

54. Beyond THC. (2013, March 30). Dabbing dangers discussed anew. Retrieved from http://www.beyondthc.com/dabbing-dangers-discussed-anew/.

55. Tashkin, D.P. (1999). Effects of marijuana on the lung and its defenses against infection and cancer. *School Psychology International, 20*(1), 23-37.

56. Singh, R. et al. (2009). Evaluation of the DNA damaging potential of cannabis cigarette smoke by the determination of acetaldehyde derived N2-ethyl-2-deoxyguanosine adducts. *Chemical Research Toxicology, 22*(6), 1181-1188.

FOOTNOTES

57. Brambilla, C. et al. (2008). Cannabis: The next villain on the lung cancer battlefield? *European Respiratory Journal, 31*(2), 227-228.

58. Berthiller, J. et al. (2008). Cannabis smoking and risk of lung cancer in men: A pooled analysis of three studies in Maghreb. *Journal Thorac Oncology, 3*(12), 1398-1403.

59. Aldington, S. et al. (2008). Cannabis use and risk of lung cancer: A case-control study. *European Respiratory Journal, 31*(2), 280-286.

60. Biello, D. (2006, May 24). Large study finds no link between marijuana and lung cancer. *Scientific American.* Retrieved from http://www.scientificamerican.com/article.cfm?id=large-study-finds-no-link.

61. Pletcher, M.J. et al. (2012). Association between marijuana exposure and pulmonary function over 20 years. *Journal of the American Medical Association, 307*(2), 173-181.

62. Zhang, Z.F. et al. (1999). Marijuana use and increased risk of squamous cell carcinoma of the head and neck. *Cancer Epidemiological Biomarkers Preview, 8*(12), 1071-1078.

63. Hashibe, M. et al. (2002). Marijuana smoking and head and neck cancer. *Journal Clinical Pharmacology, 42*(11 Suppl.), 103S-107S.

64. Hashibe, M. et al. (2002). Marijuana smoking and head and neck cancer.

MYTH 2

1. Emory Wheel Entertainment Staff. (1979, February 6). NORML chairman Keith Stroup talks on pot issues. *Emory Wheel.* Retrieved from http://www.nationalfamilies.org/legalization/redherring.html.

2. O'Connell, T. et al. (2007). Long term marijuana users seeking medical cannabis in California (2001-2007): Demographics, social characteristics, patterns of cannabis and other drug use of 4117 applicants. *Harm Reduction Journal.* Retrieved from http://www.harmreductionjournal.com/content/4/1/16.

3. Nunberg, H. et al. (2011). An analysis of applicants presenting to a medical marijuana specialty practice in California. *Journal of Drug Policy Analysis, 4*(1). Retrieved from http://www.bepress.com/jdpa/vol4/iss1/art1.

4. Cerda, M. et al. (2012). Medical marijuana laws in 50 states: Investigating the relationship between state legalization of medical marijuana and marijuana use, abuse and dependence. *Drug & Alcohol Dependence, 120*(1-3), 22-27.

5. Wall, M.M. et al. (2011). Adolescent marijuana use from 2002 to 2008: Higher in states with medical marijuana laws, cause still unclear. *Annals of Epidemiology, 21*(9), 714-716.

6. Emory Wheel Entertainment Staff (1979, February 6). NORML chairman Keith Stroup.

7. Fitzgerald, R. (2010, June 17). Will California's marijuana legalization vote radically alter our collective consciousness? *Examiner.* Retrieved from http://www.examiner.com/article/will-california-s-marijuana-legalization-vote-radically-alter-our-collective-consciousness.

8. Proper strategy in Afghanistan; wildfires in California continue; marijuana legalization. (2009, May 9) *CNN Newsroom.* [Television news program]. Retrieved from http://transcripts.cnn.com/TRANSCRIPTS/0905/09/cnr.04.html.

9. National Conference of State Legislatures. (n.d.) State medical marijuana laws. Retrieved from http://www.ncsl.org/issues-research/health/state-medical-marijuana-laws.aspx.

10. Levine, D. (1998). Funded by billionaires, the 'medical marijuana' movement is blowing smoke in our eyes. *Reader's Digest*, April 1998.

11. Pain relieving cannabis [Television series episode]. (2012). In Wallace, C. and Braverman, C. (Executive Producers), *Weed Wars.* Silver Spring, MD: The Discovery Channel. Retrieved from http://health.discovery.com/tv-shows/specials/videos/weed-wars.htm.

FOOTNOTES

12. Gorelick, D.A., and Heishman, S.J. (2006). Methods for clinical research involving marijuana administration. *Methods in molecular medicine: marijuana and cannabinoid research, methods and protocols*, *123*, 235-253.

13. National Research Council. (1999). Marijuana and medicine: Assessing the science base. Washington, D.C.: The National Academies Press.

14. Caroline on Crack. (2010, January 29). Medical marijuana edibles: More than just your big brother's pot brownie. *LA Weekly*. Retrieved from http://blogs.laweekly.com/squidink/2010/01/medical_ marijuana_edibles_more.php.

15. Caroline on Crack. (2010, January 29). Medical marijuana edibles.

16. RB. (2011, May 18). Beginner's guide to medical cannabis – using edibles. Retrieved from http://berkeleypatientscare.com/2011/05/18/ beginners-guide-to-medical-cannabis-using-edibles/.

17. RB. (2011, May 18). Beginner's guide to medical cannabis.

18. Medical Marijuana Evaluation Centers. (2009, June 22). Medical marijuana: Inhalation vs. edibles – Why is it so different? Retrieved from http://marijuanamedicine.com/2009/06/medical-marijuana- inhalation-vs-edibles-why-is-it-so-different/.

19. Fagan, K. (2012, March 3). Medical pot: S.F. seeks tighter rules on edibles. *SFGate*. Retrieved from http://www.sfgate.com/default/article/ Medical-pot-S-F-seeks-tighter-rules-on-edibles-3378765.php.

20. O'Connell, T. et al. (2007). Long term marijuana users seeking medical cannabis.

21. Nunberg, H. et al. (2011). An analysis of applicants presenting to a medical marijuana specialty practice.

22. Colorado Department of Public Health. (n.d.) Medical marijuana statistics. Retrieved from http://www.colorado.gov/cs/Satellite/CDPHE- CHEIS/CBON/1251593017044.

23. Cerda, M. et al. (2012). Medical marijuana laws in 50 states.

24. Wall, M.M. et al. (2011). Adolescent marijuana use from 2002 to 2008.

25. U.S. Department of Transportation. (2007). Results of the 2007 national roadside survey of alcohol and drug use by drivers. (Report No. DOT HS 811 175). Washington, D.C.: National Highway Traffic Safety Administration.

26. Mu-Chen, L. et al. (2012). Marijuana use and motor vehicle crashes. *Epidemiological Reviews, 34*(1), 65-72.

27. Asbridge, M. et al. (2012). Acute cannabis consumption and motor vehicle collision risk: Systematic review of observational studies and meta-analysis. *British Medical Journal, 344,* 536.

28. Landau, E. (2012, February 9). Marijuana nearly doubles risk of collisions. *CNN Health.* Retrieved from http://thechart.blogs.cnn.com/2012/02/09/marijuana-nearly-doubles-risk-of-collisions/.

29. Blows, S. et al. (2005). Marijuana use and car crash injury. *Addiction, 100*(5), 605-611.

30. Anderson, D.M., and Rees, D.I. (2011). Medical marijuana laws, traffic fatalities, and alcohol consumption. *Institute for the Study of Labor Discussion Paper No. 6112.* Retrieved from http://ssrn.com/absract=1965129.

31. Pacula, R. (2012, October). In J. Sindelar (Chair). The impact of medical marijuana policies on recreational use. Presentation delivered at the Addiction Health Services Research Conference, New York, NY; and Pacula, R. (2012, November). In P. Wilcox and J. Wooldredge (Chair). Medical marijuana and recreational marijuana use: What does and does not matter? Presentation delivered at the American Society of Criminology Conference, Chicago, IL.

32. Colorado Department of Transportation. (n.d.) Drugged driving fact sheet. Retrieved from http://www.coloradodot.info/programs/alcohol-and-impaired-driving/druggeddriving/assets/DrugFatal_

FOOTNOTES

DataasofJanuary2012.pdf.

33. Booth, M. (2013, April 1). Colorado pot accidents spur call for childproof packaging. *Denver Post*. Retrieved from http://www.denverpost.com/news/marijuana/ci_22912949/colorado-pot-accidents-spur-call-childproof-packaging#ixzz2PFANGLtw.

34. Barthwell, A.G., Baxter, Sr., L.E., Cermak, T., Kraus, M.L. and Levounis, P. (2010). The role of the physician in 'medical' marijuana. *American Society of Addiction Medicine*. Retrieved from http://www.asam.org/advocacy/find-a-policy-statement/view-policy-statement/public-policy-statements/2011/11/28/the-role-of-the-physician-in-medical-marijuana.

35. Barthwell, A.G. (2010). The role of the physician in 'medical' marijuana.

36. Hazekamp, A. et al. (2010). Review on clinical studies with cannabis and cannabinoids 2005-2009. *Cannabinoids, 5*(special issue), 1-21.

37. Barthwell, A.G. (2010). The role of the physician in 'medical' marijuana.

MYTH 3

1. Schwartz, J. (2002, August 1). Lee Otis, free. *Texas Monthly*. Retrieved from http://www.texasmonthly.com/content/lee-otis-free.

2. Olsen, C. (n.d.) The early state marijuana laws. *Schaffer Library of Drug Policy*. Retrieved from http://druglibrary.org/olsen/dpf/whitebread05.html.

3. Bonnie, R.J. and Whitebread, C.H. (1970). The genesis of marijuana prohibition. *Virginia Law Review, 56*(6).

4. Bonnie, R.J. (1970). The genesis of marijuana prohibition.

5. Peary, D. (1981). *Cult Movies*. New York: Delacorte Press.

6. Bonnie, R.J. and Whitebread, II, C.H. (1970.) The forbidden fruit

and the tree of knowledge: An inquiry into the legal history of American marijuana prohibition. *Virginia Law Review, 56*(6), 971-1203.

7. Bonnie, R.J. (1970). The forbidden fruit and the tree of knowledge.

8. Bonnie, R.J. (1970). The forbidden fruit and the tree of knowledge.

9. Bonnie, R.J. (1970). The forbidden fruit and the tree of knowledge.

10. Cooper, C. and McCullagh, D. (2009, November 10). America's love-hate history with pot. *CBS News.* Retrieved from http://www.cbsnews.com/stories/2009/07/13/national/main5154550.shtml.

11. PBS. (1998, April). Marijuana timeline. *Frontline.* Retrieved from http://www.pbs.org/wgbh/pages/frontline/shows/dope/etc/cron.html.

12. National Research Council. (1982). An analysis of marijuana policy. Washington, D.C.: The National Academies Press.

13. MSNBC. (2008, November 5). States issue verdicts on gay rights, abortion. *NBC News.* Retrieved from http://www.nbcnews.com/id/27523989/ns/politics-decision_08/t/states-issue-verdicts-gay-rights-abortion/#.UcBxqOsVzZs

14. O'Driscoll, P. (2005, November 3). Denver votes to legalize marijuana possession. *USA Today*. Retrieved from http://usatoday30.usatoday.com/news/nation/2005-11-03-pot_x.htm?csp=15.

15. NORML. (n.d.) Your government is lying to you (again) about marijuana: A refutation of the drug czar's 'open letter to America's prosecutors.' Retrieved from http://norml.org/pdf_files/your_gov_is_lying.pdf.

16. Eagan, M. (1994, September 18). Time to end smoke and mirrors on pot. *Boston Herald*.

17. Schlosser, E. (1994, August 1). Reefer madness. *The Atlantic Monthly, 274*(2), 45-63.

18. Bureau of Justice Statistics. (2004). Data collection: Survey of inmates in state correctional facilities (SISCF). Retrieved from http://www.bjs.gov/index.cfm?ty=dcdetail&iid=275.

19. Reuter, P., Hirschfield, P. and Davies, C. (2001). Assessing the

FOOTNOTES

crackdown on marijuana in Maryland. *Drug Policy Alliance*. Retrieved from http://www.drugpolicy.org/docUploads/md_mj_crackdown.pdf.

20. Caulkins, J. (2010). Cost of marijuana prohibition on the California criminal justice system, WR-763-RC. *RAND Drug Policy Research Center*.

21. Kilmer, B. et al. (2010). Altered state? Assessing how marijuana legalization in California could influence marijuana consumption and public budgets. *RAND Drug Policy Research Center*.

22. MacCoun, R.J. and Reuter, P.H. (2001). *Drug war heresies: Learning from other vices, times & places*. London: Oxford University Press.

23. Caulkins, J. and Sevigny, E. (2005). How many people does the U.S. imprison for drug use, and who are they? *Contemporary Drug Problems, 32*(3), 405-428.

24. Bureau of Justice Statistics. (2004). Data collection: Survey of inmates.

25. Caulkins, J. (2005). How many people does the U.S. imprison for drug use.

26. U.S. Sentencing Commission. (2011). 2011 annual report. Retrieved from http://www.ussc.gov/Data_and_Statistics/Annual_Reports_and_Sourcebooks/2011/ar11toc.htm.

27. U.S. Sentencing Commission. (2011). 2011 annual report.

28. U.S. Sentencing Commission. (2011). 2011 annual report.

29. U.S. Sentencing Commission. (2011). 2011 annual report.

30. Federal Bureau of Investigation. (2011). Persons arrested. Retrieved from http://www.fbi.gov/about-us/cjis/ucr/crime-in-the-u.s/2011/crime-in-the-u.s.-2011/persons-arrested.

31. Chaloupka, F.J. and Laixuthai, A. (1997). Do youths substitute alcohol and marijuana? Some econometric evidence. *Eastern Economic Journal, 23*(3), 253-276.

32. Pacula, R. (1998). Does increasing the beer tax reduce marijuana consumption? *Journal of Health Economics, 17,* 557-585.

33. Pacula, R. (1998). Adolescent alcohol and marijuana consumption: Is there really a gateway effect? *National Bureau of Economic Research*, working paper no. 6348. Retrieved from http://www.nber.org/papers/w6348.

34. Substance Abuse and Mental Health Services Administration. (2012). Results from the 2011 national survey on drug use and health: Summary of national findings. NSDUH series H-44, HHS Publication No. (SMA) 12-4713. Rockville, MD: Substance Abuse and Mental Health Services Administration.

35. National Institute of Justice. (2006). Drug courts: The second decade. Retrieved from http://www.nij.gov/pubs-sum/211081.htm.

36. Hawken, A. and Kleiman, M. (2009). Managing drug involved probationers with swift and certain sanctions: Evaluating Hawaii's HOPE. *National Institute of Justice*. Retrieved from https://www.ncjrs.gov/pdffiles1/nij/grants/229023.pdf.

37. Dupont, R.L. et al. (2009). How are addicted physicians treated? A national survey of physicians' health programs. *Journal of Substance Abuse Treatment, 37*, 1-7.

38. Kilmer, B. et al. (2013). Efficacy of frequent monitoring with swift, certain, and modest sanctions for violations: Insights from South Dakota's 24/7 sobriety project. *American Journal of Public Health*, 1. Retrieved from http://www.ncbi.nlm.nih.gov/pubmed/23153129.

39. Rossman, S.B. et al. (2011). The multi-site adult drug court evaluation: What's happening with drug courts? *A Portrait of Drug Courts in 2004, 2*. Retrieved from http://www.urban.org/publications/412355.html.

40 Kleiman, M. and Hawken, A. (2012, December). In John Q. Wilson (Chair). Managing drug involved offenders. Presentation delivered at NIJ research for the real world seminar. Retrieved from http://nij.gov/multimedia/presenter/presenter-kleiman-hawken/data/resources/presenter-kleiman-hawken-transcript.htm.

41. Kennedy, D.M. and Wong, S.L. (2009;2012). The high point

drug market intervention strategy. *U.S. Department of Justice, Office of Community Oriented Policing Services.* Retrieved from http://www.cops. usdoj.gov/Publications/e08097226-HighPoint.pdf.

42. Corsaro, N. and McGarrell, E.F. (2009). An evaluation of the Nashville drug market initiative (DMI) pulling levers strategy. *National Network for Safe Communities.* Retrieved from http://www. nnscommunities.org/NashvilleEvaluation.pdf.

MYTH 4

1. For more information on this statistic, see Harwood, H. (2000). Updating estimates of the economic costs of alcohol abuse in the United States: Estimates, update methods, and data. Report prepared for the National Institute on Alcohol Abuse and Alcoholism. Retrieved from http://pubs.niaaa.nih.gov/publications/economic-2000/; Urban Institute and Brookings Institution (2012, October 15). State and local alcoholic beverage tax revenue, selected years 1977-2010. *Tax Policy Center.* Retrieved from http://www.taxpolicycenter.org/taxfacts/ displayafact.cfm?Docid=399; Saul, S. (2008, August 30). Government gets hooked on tobacco tax billions. *The New York Times.* Retrieved from http://www.nytimes.com/2008/08/31/weekinreview/31saul. html?em&_r=0; for Federal estimates, see Urban Institute and Brookings Institution (2012, October 15). State and local tobacco tax revenue, selected years 1977-2010. *Tax Policy Center.* Retrieved from http://www. taxpolicycenter.org/taxfacts/displayafact.cfm?Docid=403; Campaign for Tobacco-Free Kids (n.d.). Toll of tobacco in the United States of America. Retrieved from http://www.tobaccofreekids.org/research/factsheets/ pdf/0072.pdf.

2. Rosenwald, M. (2010, October 30). The year is 2020: What's happening with marijuana. *Washington Post.* Retrieved from http:// www.washingtonpost.com/wp-dyn/content/article/2010/10/22/

AR2010102205573.html?sid=ST2010102805974.

3. Smith, R. (2012, November 17). Marijuana legalization: 3 legit angles to profit from decriminalized pot. Daily Finance. Retrieved from http://www.dailyfinance.com/2012/11/17/marijuana-legalization-3-legit-angles-to-profit-from-decriminal/.

4. McLaurin, J. and Osifekun, O.B. (2002, November 13). Strategy paper: Is Phillip Morris a good fit for mary jane? Internal document for California Institute of Technology. Retrieved from http://www.mcafee.cc/Classes/BEM106/Papers/UTexas/351/Phillipmorris.pdf.

5. Young, C. (2013, May 28). Former Microsoft manager has big ideas about marketing retail pot, The Seattle Times. Retrieved from http://seattletimes.com/html/localnews/2021075621_potshivelyxml.html.

6. Brief of Amici Curiae Tobacco Control Legal Consortium, Roswell Park Cancer Institute, and Professor Harry Lando in Support of United States et al., in Support of Affirmance in Part and Reversal in Part. Discount Tobacco City & Lottery, Inc., et al. v. United States of America, et al. 10-5234. (6th Cir. U.S. Court of Appeals, 2010).

7. The Legacy Foundation. (n.d.) Secret documents, young people and smoking: Document #167. Retrieved from http://www.legacy.library.ucsf.edu/tid/doq76b00/pdf.

8. The Legacy Foundation. (n.d.) Secret documents.

9. *Statement of David Goerlitz, former model for Winston cigarettes, on behalf of the Coalition on Smoking or Health*, Washington, D.C. (1989, April 13). Retrieved from http://www.legacy.library.ucsf.edu/action/document/page?tid=lpm40c00&page=1.

10. Kleiman, M., Caulkins, J.P. and Hawken, A. (2011). *Drugs and drug policy: What everyone needs to know*. Oxford: Oxford University Press.

11. Kleiman, M. (2011). *Drugs and drug policy*.

12. Kleiman, M. (2010, August 13). Against commercial cannabis. *The Reality-Based Community*. Retrieved from http://www.samefacts.com/2010/08/drug-policy/against-commercial-cannabis/.

FOOTNOTES

13. Cook, P.J. and Tauchen, G. (1982). The effect of liquor taxes on heavy drinking. *Bell Journal of Economics, 13*(2), 379-390.

14. Kleiman, M., Caulkins, J.P. and Hawken, A. (2011) *Drugs and drug policy.*

15. Jones-Webb, R. et al. (2008). Alcohol and malt liquor availability and promotion and homicide in inner cities. *Substance Use & Misuse, 43*(2), 159-177.

16. Moore, M.M. (1989, October 16). Actually, prohibition was a success. *The New York Times.* Retrieved from http://www.nytimes.com/1989/10/16/opinion/actually-prohibition-was-a-success.html.

17. Kleber, H., Califano, J. and Demers, J. (2005). Clinical and societal implications of drug legalization. In Lowinson, R., Millman, and Langrod (Eds.), *Substance Abuse: A Comprehensive Textbook* (4th ed.) Baltimore: Williams and Wilkins.

18. Kilmer, B. et al. (2010). Reducing drug trafficking revenues and violence in Mexico: Would legalizing marijuana in California help? *RAND International Programs and Drug Policy Research Center.*

19. Kilmer, B. et al. (2010). Reducing drug trafficking revenues and violence, p. 3.

20. Kilmer, B. et al. (2010). Reducing drug trafficking revenues and violence, p. 3.

21. Kilmer, B. et al. (2010). Reducing drug trafficking revenues and violence, p. 30.

22. Hope, A. and Clark. E. (2012). Si los vecinos legalizan: Reporte técnico. *IMCO.* Retrieved from http://imco.org.mx/wp-content/uploads/2012/10/reporte_tecnico_legalizacion_marihuana.pdf; English explanation retrieved from http://imco.org.mx/wp-content/uploads/2012/10/clarification.pdf; English commentary by Hope, A. retrieved from http://www.samefacts.com/2012/12/drug-policy/polarization-denial-and-the-cannabis-debate/.

23. e.g. June S. Beittel, *Mexico's Drug Trafficking Organizations: Source and Scope of the Rising Violence, Congressional Research Service* (CRS) Report for Congress, 7-7500. June 7, 2011.

MYTH 5

1. Okrent, D. (2010). *Last call: The rise and fall of prohibition.* New York: Scribner.

2. Montopoli, B. (2009, March 26). Obama: Legalizing pot won't grow economy. *CBS News.* Retrieved from http://www.cbsnews.com/8301-503544_162-4894639-503544.html.

3. *Legalizing marijuana: Issues to consider before reforming California state law*: Hearing before the California State Assembly Public Safety Committee, (2009, October 28)(testimony of Rosalie Pacula).

4. Kilmer, B. et al. (2010). Altered state? Assessing how marijuana legalization in California could influence marijuana consumption and public budgets. *RAND Drug Policy Research Center.*

5. Smith, G. and Wynne, H. (1999). Gambling and crime in western Canada: Exploring myth and reality. Report prepared for the Canada West Foundation. Retrieved from http://cwf.ca/pdf-docs/publications/September1999-Summary-Report-Gambling-and-Crime-in-Western-Canada.pdf.

6. Kilmer, B. et al. (2010). Altered state, p. 23.

7. MacCoun, R.J. and Reuter, P.H. (2001). *Drug war heresies: Learning from other vices, times & places.* London: Oxford University Press.

8. Kilmer, B. et al. (2010). Altered state.

9. Pacula testimony, *Legalizing marijuana.*

10. Pacula, R. et al. (2008, June). *An examination of the nature and cost of marijuana treatment episodes.* Working paper presented at the American Society for Health Economics Annual Meeting, Durham, NC.

11. Ingold, J. (2013, March 28). Scathing audit throws Colorado

recreational marijuana rules into chaos. *Denver Post*. Retrieved from http://www.denverpost.com/breakingnews/ci_22890505/ scathing-audit-throws-colorado-recreational-marijuana-rules-into#ixzz2OzEzdmho.

12. Jossens, L. and Raw, M. (2000). How can cigarette smuggling be reduced? *British Medical Journal, 321,* 945-950.

13. Fitz, J. (2007). California cigarette excise tax revenue loss estimates. Presentation at the Federation of Tax Administrators Revenue Estimating and Tax Research Conference. Retrieved from http://www.taxadmin.org/fta/meet/07rev_est/papers/fitz.pdf.

14. Fitz, J. (2007). California cigarette excise tax revenue loss estimates.

15. LaFaive, M.D. et al. (2008). *Cigarette taxes and smuggling: A statistical analysis and historical review*. Midland, MI: Mackinac Center for Public Policy.

16. Watson, B. (2010, April 20). Pot economics: Who stands to profit if marijuana is legalized? *Daily Finance*. Retrieved from http://www.dailyfinance.com/2010/04/20/pot-economics-who-stands-to-profit-if-marijuana-is-legalized/.

MYTH 6

1. Darrall, S. (2011, October 8). Dutch government bans coffee-shops from selling 'skunk.' *Daily Mail*. Retrieved from http://www.dailymail.co.uk/news/article-2046768/Dutch-government-bans-coffee-shops-selling-skunk.html.

2. Specter, M. (2011, October 17). Getting a fix: Portugal decriminalized drugs a decade ago; what have we learned? *The New Yorker*. Retrieved from http://www.newyorker.com/reporting/2011/10/17/111017fa_fact_specter.

3. For more on these articles, see Sloan, J. (2012, July 20). Ten years

of legalization has cut Portugal's drug abuse rate in half. *Disinformation.* Retrieved from http://disinfo.com/2012/07/ten-years-of-legalization-has-cut-portugals-drug-abuse-rate-in-half/; The Huffington Post. (2011, November 12). What happened after Portugal made all drugs legal? Retrieved from http://www.huffingtonpost.com/2011/07/13/portugal-legal-drugs_n_897207.html; Regan, T. (2011, April 20). What pot legalization looks like. *The Huffington Post.* Retrieved from http://www.huffingtonpost.com/trish-regan/what-pot-legalization-loo_b_851550.html.

4. Greenwald, G. (2009, April 2). Drug decriminalization in Portugal: Lessons for creating fair and successful drug policies. *Cato Institute.* Retrieved from http://www.cato.org/publications/white-paper/drug-decriminalization-portugal-lessons-creating-fair-successful-drug-policies.

5. Chivers, T. (2010, September 28). Portugal drug decriminalization 'a resounding success': Will Britain respond? No. *Telegraph.* Retrieved from http://blogs.telegraph.co.uk/culture/tomchivers/100047485/portugal-drug-decriminalisation-a-resounding-success-will-britain-respond-no/.

6. Greenwald, G. (2010, October 14). Drug decriminalization policy pays off. *Politico.* http://www.cato.org/publications/commentary/drug-decriminalization-policy-pays.

7. Vastag, B. (2009, April 7). 5 years after: Portugal's drug decriminalization policy shows positive results. *Scientific American.* Retrieved from http://www.scientificamerican.com/article.cfm?id=portugal-drug-decriminalization.

8. Specter, M. (2011). Getting a fix, p. 37.

9. European Monitoring Centre for Drugs and Drug Addiction (EMCDDA). (2013, May 27). Country overview: Portugal. Retrieved from http://www.emcdda.europa.eu/publications/country-overviews/pt#drd.

FOOTNOTES

10. EMCDDA. (2013, May 27). Country overview.

11. Vale de Andrade, P. (2010). Drug decriminalization in Portugal. *British Medical Journal, 341,* c4554. Retrieved from http://www.bmj.com/content/341/bmj.c4554.

12. EMCDDA. (2013, May 27). Country overview.

13. Humphreys, K. (2010). Scientific proof that drug decriminalization in Portugal saved lives and killed people. *The Reality-Based Community*. Retrieved from http://www.samefacts.com/2010/10/drug-policy/scientific-proof-that-drug-decriminalization-in-portugal-saved-lives-and-killed-people/.

14. EMCDDA. (2011). Drug policy profiles – Portugal. Lisbon: EMCDDA, p. 24.

15. Specter, M. (2011). Getting a fix, p. 44.

16. Collins, L. (1999). Holland's half-baked drug experiment. *Foreign Affairs*. Retrieved from http://www.foreignaffairs.com/articles/55014/larry-collins/hollands-half-baked-drug-experiment.

17. Collins, L. (1999). Holland's half-baked drug experiment.

18. MacCoun, R.J. and Reuter, P.H. (2001). *Drug war heresies: Learning from other vices, times & places*. London: Oxford University Press.

19. EMCDDA. (2008). *A cannabis reader: Global issues and local experiences*. Lisbon: EMCDDA.

20. EMCDDA. (2008). *A cannabis reader*.

21. MacCoun, R.J. and Reuter, P.H. (2001). *Drug war heresies*.

22. EMCDDA. (2008). *A cannabis reader*.

23. EMCDDA. (2009) Table TDI-3: New clients entering treatment by primary drug, 1997 to 2007, part IV: New cannabis clients by country and year of treatment. *Statistical Bulletin 2009: Treatment Demand Indicator*. Lisbon: EMCDDA.

24. Collins, L. (1999). Holland's half-baked drug experiment.

25. Collins, L. (1999). Holland's half-baked drug experiment.

26. LeFever, R. (2011, October 11). Even the Dutch think skunk drives you mad. *Daily Mail*. Retrieved from http://www.dailymail.co.uk/debate/article-2047750/The-grass-greener-Holland.html.

27. British Broadcasting Corporation. (2012, April 27). Netherlands judge backs café cannabis ban. *BBC News Europe*. Retrieved from http://www.bbc.co.uk/news/world-europe-17865151.

MYTH 7

1. Shuman, H.E. (1987, October 22). Interview by Donald A. Ritchie. Interview #10: Heroes and Theories, United States Historical Office. Retrieved from http://www.senate.gov/artandhistory/history/resources/pdf/Shuman_interview_10.pdf.

2. Office of National Drug Control Policy. (n.d.) Marijuana resource center. Retrieved from http://www.whitehouse.gov/ondcp/marijuanainfo.

3. Marijuana Potency Monitoring Program, University of Mississippi. (2011, December 19). *Quarterly Report #115*.

4. Office of Applied Studies, DASIS Series: S-45. (2007). Treatment episode data set highlights – 2007, national admission to substance abuse treatment services. *DHHS Publication* No. SMA 09-4360.

5. National Institute on Drug Abuse (NIDA). (2003). *Preventing drug use among children and adolescents: A research-based guide for parents, educators, and community leaders, Second edition.* NIH Publication No. 04-4212(A).

6. NIDA. (2003). *Preventing drug use among children and adolescents.*

7. NIDA. (2011). Drugfacts: Lessons from prevention research. Retrieved from http://www.drugabuse.gov/publications/drugfacts/lessons-prevention-research.

8. Kliewer, W. and Murrelle, L. (2007). Risk and protective factors for adolescent substance use: Findings from a study in selected Central

FOOTNOTES

American countries. *Journal of Adolescent Health, 40,* 448-455.

9. Cheng, T.C. and Lo, C.C. (2011). A longitudinal analysis of some risk and protective factors in marijuana use by adolescents receiving child welfare services. *Children and Youth Services Review, 33,* (1667-1672).

10. Humensky, J.L. (2010). Are adolescents with high socioeconomic status more likely to engage in alcohol and illicit drug use in early adulthood? *Substance Abuse Treatment, Prevention, and Policy, 5,* 19-28.

11. Legleye, S. et al. (2011). Social gradient in initiation and transition to daily use of tobacco and cannabis during adolescence: A retrospective cohort study. *Addiction, 106,* 1520-1531.

12. Johnston, L.D., O'Malley, P.M., Bachman, J.G. and Schulenberg, J.E. (2011). *Monitoring the future national survey results on drug use, 1975-2010: Volume I, Secondary school students.* Ann Arbor: Institute for Social Research, The University of Michigan.

13. NIDA. (2003). *Preventing drug use among children and adolescents.*

14. NIDA. (2003). *Preventing drug use among children and adolescents.*

15. Hall, W. and Pacula, R. (2003). *Cannabis use and dependence: Public health and public policy.* Melbourne, Australia: Cambridge University Press.

16. Snell-Johns, J. et al. (2003). Roles assumed by a community coalition when creating environmental and policy-level changes. *Journal of Community Psychology, 31*(6), 661-670.

17. Goode, E. (2001). *Drugs in American society* (8th ed.). New York, NY: McGraw-Hill.

18. Community Anti-Drug Coalitions of America (CADCA). (2012). Senate sign-on letter. Retrieved from http://www.cadca.org/files/FinalFY%2013SignedSenateFinal.pdf.

19. CADCA. (2012). Senate sign-on letter.

20. CADCA. (2012). Senate sign-on letter.

21. Office of National Drug Control Policy (ONDCP). (2010). National evaluation of the drug free communities support program summary of

findings through 2010. Retrieved from http://www.whitehouse.gov/
sites/default/files/ondcp/grants-content/2011_dfc_interim_report_one_
pager_final.pdf.

22. Previously published research includes: Snell-Johns, J. et al.
(2003). Roles assumed.; Sorenson, G. et al. (1998). Implications of the
results of community intervention trials. *Annual Review of Public Health,*
19, 379-416; Mazerolle, L., Soole, D.W. and Rombouts, S. (2007). *Crime*
prevention research reviews no. 1: Disrupting street-level drug markets.
Washington, D.C.: U.S. Department of Justice, Office of Community
Oriented Policing Services.

23. Mayet, A. et al. (2012). Cannabis use stages as predictors of
subsequent initiation with other illicit drugs among French adolescents:
Use of a multi-state model. *Addictive Behaviours, 37*(2), 161-166.

24. Fiellin, L. et al. (2013). Previous use of alcohol, cigarettes, and
marijuana and subsequent abuse of prescription opioids in young adults.
Journal of Adolescent Health, 52(2), 158-163.

25. Lynskey, M.T. et al. (2003). Escalation of drug use in early-onset
cannabis users vs. co-twin controls. *Journal of the American Medical*
Association, 289(4), 427-433.

26. MacCoun, R.J. and Reuter, P.H. (2001). *Drug war heresies:*
Learning from other vices, times & places. London: Oxford University
Press.

27. Dupre, D. (1995). Initiation and progression of alcohol,
marijuana and cocaine use among adolescent abusers. *American Journal*
of Addiction, 4, 43-48.

28. Simmons, R., Conger, R., and Whitbeck, L. (1998). A multistage
reaming model of the influences of family and peers upon adolescent
substance abuse. *Journal of Drug Issues, 18*(3), 293-315.

29. Fiellin, L. et al. (2013). Previous use of alcohol, cigarettes, and
marijuana.

30. NIDA. (2012, December). Drugfacts: Marijuana. Retrieved from

FOOTNOTES

http://www.drugabuse.gov/publications/drugfacts/marijuana.

31. Psychology Today. (n.d.) Cognitive behavioral therapy. Retrieved from http://www.psychologytoday.com/basics/cognitive-behavioral-therapy.

32. NIDA. (2012, December). *Principles of drug addiction treatment: A research-based guide* (3rd ed.) Retrieved from http://www.drugabuse.gov/publications/principles-drug-addiction-treatment.

33. Carroll, K.M. et al. (2005). Behavioral therapies for drug abuse. *American Journal of Psychiatry, 162,* 1452-1460.

34. NIDA. (2012, December). *Principles of drug addiction treatment.*

35. Carroll, K.M. et al. (2006). The use of contingency management and motivational/skills-building therapy to treat young adults with cannabis dependence. *Journal of Consulting and Clinical Psychology,* 74(5), 955-966.

36. NIDA. (2012, December). *Principles of drug addiction treatment.*

37. Budney, A.J. et al. (2006). Clinical trial of abstinence-based vouchers and cognitive-behavioral therapy for cannabis dependence. *Journal of Consulting and Clinical Psychology,* 74(2), 307-316.

38. Calabria, B. et al. (2010). Systematic review of prospective studies investigating 'remission' from amphetamine, cannabis, cocaine or opioid dependence. *Addictive Behaviors, 35,* 741-749.

BIOGRAPHIC SUMMARY OF

KEVIN A. SABET, PH.D.

Dubbed the "quarterback" of the new anti-drug movement by *Salon Magazine*, Kevin A. Sabet, Ph.D has over 18 years experience working on drug policy. Dr. Sabet is the Director of the Drug Policy Institute at the University of Florida and an Assistant Professor in the College of Medicine, Department of Psychiatry. With Patrick J. Kennedy, he is the co-founder of Project SAM (Smart Approaches to Marijuana). He is also a policy consultant to numerous domestic and international organizations through his company, the Policy Solutions Lab.

Representing his non-partisan commitment to drug policy, he previously worked on research, policy, and speech writing at the White House Office of National Drug Control Policy (ONDCP) in 2000 and from 2003-2004 in the Clinton and Bush Administrations, respectively. From 2009-2011, he served in the Obama Administration as the Senior Advisor to Director Kerlikowske at the ONDCP.

In his most recent senior position, Dr. Sabet advised Director Kerlikowske on all matters affecting priorities, policies, and programs of the National Drug Control Strategy. He was one of three main writers of President Obama's first National Drug Control

Strategy, and his portfolio included leading the office's efforts on marijuana policy, legalization issues, international demand reduction, drugged driving, and synthetic drug (e.g. "Spice" and "Bath Salts") policy.

Dr. Sabet is a staff columnist at TheFix.com and a regular contributor to opinion-editorial pages worldwide, including the *Washington Post, Huffington Post, New York Times, Vancouver Sun, San Francisco Chronicle, Seattle Times*, CNN, CNBC, and more than a dozen other media outlets. His first editorial since leaving ONDCP, published in the *Los Angeles Times* in September of 2011, earned him a "Five Best Columns" distinction by *The Atlantic.*

As a Marshall Scholar, he received his Ph.D. and M.S. in Social Policy at Oxford University and B.A. in Political Science from the University of California, Berkeley. He currently lives in Cambridge, Massachusetts with his wife, Shahrzad.

.